PHENOMENAL
Woman

The Dora Stockman Story

By Margaret O'Rourke-Kelly, Ph.D.

ZOË LIFE
PUBLISHING
WORDS TO LIVE BY

Published by:
Zoë Life Publishing
P.O. Box 871066
Canton, MI 48187 USA
www.zoelifepub.com

Author: Margaret O'Rourke-Kelly, Ph.D.
Cover Designer: Chamira Jones
Editors: Jessica Colvin, Scott Memmer

First U.S. Edition 2008

Library of Congress Cataloging-in-Publication Data

O'Rourke-Kelly, Margaret.
  Phenomenal women : the Dora Stockman story / by Margaret O'Rourke-Kelly.
– 1st U.S. ed.
    p. cm.
  Includes bibliographical references.
  ISBN 978-1-934363-18-8 (soft cover)
  1. Stockman, Dora Hall, 1872-1948. 2. Social reformers–Michigan–Biography. 3. Women social reformers–Michigan–Biography. 4. Michigan State Grange–Biography. 5. State governments–Officials and employees. 6. Politicians–Michigan–Biography. 7. Women politicians–Michigan–Biography. 8. College teachers–Michigan–Biography. 9. Women college teachers–Michigan–Biography. 10. Michigan–Biography.
  I. Title.
  CT275.S77A3 2008
  977.4'043092–dc22
  [B]
                            2007039367

10 Digit ISBN 1-934363-18-9 Soft cover, Perfect Bound
13 Digit ISBN 978-1-934363-18-8 Soft cover, Perfect Bound

For current information about releases by Margaret O'Rourke-Kelly, Ph.D. or other releases from Zoë Life Publishing, visit our web site: http://www.zoelifepub.com

Printed in the United States of America

v12 05 23 08

Acknowledgments

My hope is to contribute to the rich harvest provided by contemporary women's studies in the life of this nation. Dora Stockman was a remarkable pioneering woman who should not be forgotten in the history of Michigan.

I initially encountered Dora Stockman when I ran for the Michigan State House of Representatives from the 2nd District of Ingham County some forty years following Dora's more successful elections from that same district. While I did not prevail in the election, a moment of serendipity occurred when I discovered the long forgotten archival records of this remarkable woman. I had been told by Tom Klunzinger that a woman had run in that district years earlier. While I was seeking background material on Dora's election campaigns, I discovered her plays for the Grange. I vowed at that moment that I would one day return and study her writing. As part of my election campaign, Thomas Rasmusson, Joseph Warren, and I collaborated to create a greeting card highlighting Dora Stockman's political and educational accomplishments. I have focused my educational research for several years on the Grange writer's life and times.

It is my goal to continue to tell Dora Stockman's story in the hope that it may inspire others to see the possible opportunities for service in their own corners of the world. It has been my privilege to study this remarkable woman. I have focused my doctoral work on the analysis of her plays and have created a one-woman show about her life and times.

Research is rarely conducted in a vacuum and this historical study was no exception. The following libraries provided a wellspring of resources and information for which I am very grateful: The Bentley Historical Library, University of Michigan at Ann Arbor, the Archives at Hillsdale College and the Hillsdale Public Library in Hillsdale, Michigan. Also the University Archives Historical Collection at Michigan State University, East Lansing, the State of Michigan Library in Lansing, Michigan, Manistee Historical Society in Manistee, Michigan, and the Benzonia Historical Society of Benzonia, Michigan.

I appreciate the support of the many men and women of the Grange who encouraged my interest in the story of Dora Stockman. Olie and Helen White encouraged me to stay at their farm for a real farm feeling. The gifts of Grange songbooks edited by Dora were given to me by members of the Benzonia Grange. Dora's son, Verne Stockman was kind enough to permit my interview with him in Glen Arbor, Michigan and Calvin Stockman and his wife Judy were gracious in attending the one-woman show and granting me several interviews. Reva Lipps and her daughter, Barbara, granted me another visit and helpful family photos.

I want to especially thank my first readers who were enthusiastic in supporting my work and providing helpful suggestions: Marsha Daigle-Williamson, Ph.D., David Deupree, Linda Emptage, M.A., Georgia Kelly, M.A, and Robert McTyre, Ph.D. Any errors are my own.

My children were also a constant source of inspiration— thank you, Margaret and David. The encouragement from my spouse, Jerry Kelly, was splendid. Finally, I want to thank family and friends for enduring yet another story about Dora Stockman as I continued to make discoveries about this remarkable woman over the last twenty years.

It is my hope that my research will encourage others to explore the vast uncharted legacy of Dora Stockman's influence in the world. She truly was a phenomenal woman.

PHENOMENAL
Woman

The Dora Stockman Story

By Margaret O'Rourke-Kelly, Ph.D.

Contents

Introduction

Little has been noted or written of Eudora Stockman, more popularly known as Dora or Mrs. Stockman, the first woman elected to state-wide public office in Michigan. A plaque on a traffic island across from Agricultural Hall at Michigan State University, in East Lansing, Michigan, notes her contributions to the university. She has received limited public acclaim for her fifty plus years working on behalf of family health and education. Yet her legacy continues in health care reforms, education and the arts.

Archival records are all that tangibly remain of this unique Michigan woman. She is an often over-looked social reformer who contributed to the richness of community life as an elected public official, newspaper editor, educator, evangelist, lecturer and writer of plays, poetry, and songs. This book explores her life's journey as seen through the lens of the life-long member of an agrarian organization. The view is a story of a woman of exceptional accomplishments and drive often at odds with the mainstream expectations for a woman of her era.

Long before today's popular culture included public forums for discussion of the family life, there was the Grange or Order of the Patrons of Husbandry to serve as a focal point for community life in rural and later urban America. In the last half of the nineteenth century, economic social conditions of the American farmer altered dramatically. The Patrons of Husbandry was formed in an effort to save the institution of the family farm. Their organizing formula soon resulted in a national rural landscape dotted with white clapboard buildings known as Grange halls.

Embracing the noble purposes of the Grange, Eudora

Stockman (1872-1948) became a champion for the cause of not only the farm family but families everywhere who struggled for education, dignity, and the American Dream. Beginning with her early years in Northern Michigan, Dora Hall joined the family in the community of active Grangerism. A historical biographical sketch of her life explores contemporary social and political life at the turn of the century in Michigan. These early foundational years gave rise to a life-time of writing and service to the community.

Educational pursuits continued during marriage and motherhood. These early married years reveal the concerns of alcohol abuse in the nearby lumbering community where the Stockman general store was established. Dora's initial college degree was first earned at Benzonia Academy. In addition, involvement in the Temperance Movement and study at the Moody Bible Institute continued to influence the writing and commitment of Dora Stockman.

Changes in her husband's health force an alteration in plans and the Stockmans began their travels leaving Northern Michigan at the turn of the century for the dry climate of western states. Upon her return to Michigan, Dora completed additional degree work and teaching at Hillsdale College. Early identified publishing efforts blossomed during this period and continued throughout her life.

Through participation in the Patrons of Husbandry, Dora was able to travel and spread the gospel of the Grange. The Grange provided an excellent vehicle for promotion, publication and study. By the time she was elected to the State Board of Agriculture in 1919 she had built a foundation of support throughout the eighty-three counties in the State of Michigan. Prior to the national women's suffrage, Dora Stockman was the first woman elected to state-wide public office in Michigan. She served on the State Board of Agriculture for two terms.

While serving on the board she continued working for the Grange and created a radio talk show, wrote and read poems, plays, pageants, and songs. Historical achievements for Stockman include the awarding of an honorary doctor of law's degree from Michigan State College in 1934 for her contributions to the college. She continued to contribute to the newspaper for the State Grange and began a doctoral degree. Within the Grange people wondered what she would do when defeated in a bid for the highest office with the Michigan Patron's of Husbandry. The wondering was short-lived.

Well-known after twelve years on the Agricultural Board, Dora Stockman had established a constituency that supported her run for the State Legislature in Lansing, Michigan's capital city. At sixty-five, an age when others consider retiring, Mrs. Stockman, now widowed began her work for the State of Michigan. She won her first election campaign for the State House. Her four terms as a state representative from East Lansing, Michigan suggest her ability to shape issues, develop constituency, and create a consensus while serving in the State House from 1938 through 1946.

Stockman was an active participant and change agent for the Patrons of Husbandry. Her unique use of drama and song inculcated generations with a zeal for mission. Discovering Dora's fascinating journey leads the reader through the bleak life of family farming to the State Legislature of Michigan. Encountering along the way a unique individual who published, promoted, and proselytized for the causes that have shaped public policy in health care reforms, education and taxation in the State of Michigan is a joy. Dora Stockman—one extraordinary woman quite at home on the Grange!

Finding Dora Stockman

While I was a candidate for state representative in East Lansing, Michigan, I learned that a woman had run for State office from the same district some forty years earlier. A visit to the Michigan State University Historical Archives opened the door to Dora Stockman. As I initially searched for her campaign material, a moment of serendipity occurred. Yes, the campaign newspaper articles and speeches were on file, but what amazed me was the wealth of material including music, poems, scripts, and plays. Her unfinished doctoral thesis on rural sociology together with her speeches were captivating. I knew that one day I would return to these archival materials.

What started with a review of her campaign material evolved into a doctoral degree and one-woman show inspired by Dora Stockman's life and times. Along the way, I discovered the interesting intersections of my life with events and places in Dora's life.

Dora Stockman is interred at Hurd Cemetery in Lansing, Michigan. As I studied her headstone, I noticed how close the Capitol City Airport was in relation to the cemetery. This is the same airport where I had taken flight lessons and where, as a student pilot, I completed the requisite seven solo takeoffs and landings.

When I found her radio ads and learned that she was the Sunshine Lady over WKAR in East Lansing, I reflected that this was the same radio station where I had served as a volunteer writer and reader.

Dora is a study in life-long learning. My life has been dedicated to life-long learning. Her wide array of interests felt so similar to my own. Since discovering Dora, I have dedicated myself to telling her story. Initially, there was skepticism. Now,

however, she has been inducted into the Michigan Women's Hall of Fame. Her contributions to families can now be shared with an even wider audience.

1

The Early Years
1872-1888

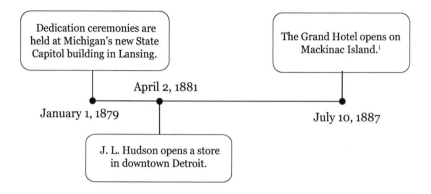

Dedication ceremonies are held at Michigan's new State Capitol building in Lansing.

The Grand Hotel opens on Mackinac Island.[1]

April 2, 1881

January 1, 1879

July 10, 1887

J. L. Hudson opens a store in downtown Detroit.

The Michigan wilderness was a destination for many families from the Eastern seaboard who sought to carve out their future in farming the rich land of the Traverse Bay, Michigan, area following the Civil War. What has now become a vacation spot for Midwesterners was at one time a wilderness evolving into a center of commerce for logging and mining operations. Railroads crisscrossed the landscape and waterways were used to transport the results of mining operations in the Manistee community in the Northern Lower Peninsula.

Wilderness Settlers

Lucy J. and Leander F. Hall followed the path of previous travelers and made their way to the Eastern shores of Lake

---

[1] *This Date in Michigan History.*

Marilla County Outline. *Source: Manistee County Historical Museum.*

Michigan. The Halls arrived in the county of Manistee in 1869 traveling by covered wagon from the Albany, New York, area and quickly became woven into the newly emerging community fabric. They settled into Marillia Township only three years after it was established in 1866. They discovered a bountiful harvest of Michigan trees including maple, beech, and pine. Leander F. Hall was among the first elected township officers. Dora's father was one of two justices of the peace for Marilla Township, Manistee County, Michigan, in 1870.[2]

According to family sources, the Hall family was a lively group of individuals who enjoyed spirited discussions, and community participation. Dora's parents are described as virtuous, temperate, and eager to provide an education for their children. Dora's mother read aloud and sang while pregnant with her. Dora Stockman said of her father, "He did not drink, swear, or use tobacco. His personal morality was unusual. He did not accumulate much money for he spent it helping his children get an education and for home advancement."[3]

The Hall family lived and worked on eighty acres near Lemon Lake in the Northwestern quadrant of the township. According to the 1880 Agricultural Census, the value of the farm was placed at $800 with the state equalized value (or SEV)

---

[2] *The Salt City of the Inland Seas.*　　　　[3] D. Stockman, *The Story of Myself.*

at $400.[4] The family of three included her father, Leander L. (1837–1919); mother, Lucy J. (1843–1905); and sister, Mina. On August 4, 1872, Eudora Hall was born, as she described it, "in a log house in Marilla Township," Manistee County, Michigan. She was called Dora from a very young age. Two

Hall Family headstone. *Source: author's personal collection.*

more children followed and, at the time of the 1880 census, the records of the Hall family showed a younger brother, Welcome F. Hall, and a younger sister, Phebe J. Hall, completing the immediate family.[5]

The Hall family tree shows a legacy of early pioneer American stock. A variety of historical family exploits include participation in tossing tea in Boston Harbor and performance as a drummer in the War of 1812. Dora's relatives also included a circuit preacher, a senator, artists, and an actress. In *The Story of Myself, 1872–1948*, Hall-Stockman provides a chronological overview of her life. This story contains the clues as to her interest and drives which led her far from the place of her birth and into a fruitful public life.

> I come of early pioneer American stock. On my paternal side, the Halls were among the group that threw the tea overboard at the Boston Tea Party. Later, part of the family moved to Vermont. From there, my paternal grandfather enlisted as a boy of fourteen in the war of

---

[4] Manistee County Directory.

[5] D. Stockman, *The Story of Myself*

1812, as a drummer. My great uncles were a circuit preacher and a senator. On my paternal mother's side, the family is of Dutch descent; the Van Reusalen family and Treush Hugrienot were related to Sarah Bernhan [sic], the French Actress.[6]

Talent, creativity, and adventure were apparent not only the father's side of her family but on her mother's side as well.

On my maternal side, the Bennets, my grandfather was Scotch-English, an artist of considerable ability who painted pictures of angels and forth in some famous churches, in Chicago before the fire. Grandfather died when I was four. My maternal grandmother was of Irish stock; thrifty and laughingly lovable.[7]

At that time the Marilla Township population was reported at 133 citizens according to Manistee County records. The township history notes, "the first school in the new township

was taught by Mrs. Jennie Pope, who continued to teach for several terms."[8] The school district increased for the township and it was noted that "Two of the school buildings are especially fine, costing about $1,000 each. The town has a well-filled public library, which speaks

Downtown Manistee with both autos and horse-drawn buggies. *Source: Manistee County Historical Museum.*

---

[6] D. Stockman, *The Story of Myself*

[7] D. Stockman, *The Story of Myself*

[8] *The Salt City of the Inland Seas*

well for the enterprise and intelligence of the people."[9]

While the township may have been in its infancy, the county held the larger city of Manistee, which was flourishing. Manistee is also the county seat and well situated on the Manistee River with access to Lake Michigan. With the discovery of rock salt reserves and numerous lumbering operations, future economic growth seemed assured. In the year of Dora Hall's birth in 1872, telegraph communications were established. By 1873, Manistee had a population of 5,000.[10] In a thriving city, entertainment, churches, volunteer organizations, public service, public utilities, schools, transportation, fraternal organizations, retailing, and professional services flourished.

Life in a smaller rural township generally revolved around home, school and church. Church societies in the area included the Congregationalists 1872 and (a few years later) the Baptists arrived in the community in 1876. The township church history notes the first person baptized by immersion in the town took place in 1876.[11] Added to that constellation was the social cooperative organization of the Grange.

Growing Up Granger

Coincidental to Dora's birth year, Michigan began its order of the Patrons of Husbandry in 1872, Susan B. Anthony was arrested,[12] and actress Maude Adams was also born.[13] Only two years later, in 1874, her parents joined the local Grange.[14] The Patrons of Husbandry were formed to combat the powerful lobbying interests in Washington, D.C., that were well

---

[9] *The Salt City of the Inland Seas*
[10] *The Salt City of the Inland Seas*
[11] *The Salt City of the Inland Seas*

[12] Gurko 250, 251
[13] Franck and Brownstone 173
[14] D. Stockman, *The Story of Myself*

Application for Membership.

To the Officers and Members of .... Grange No. ....

of the Patrons of Husbandry:

I, ... a resident of the town of

...., County of .... and State of ....

being .... years of age, and by occupation a ...., respectfully
petition to be initiated a member of your Order.

    In presenting this petition I am influenced by no other motive than by a desire to unite with
others in elevating and advancing the interests of Husbandry, and receive in return such benefits as
may accrue to all who belong to the Order.

    Should my petition be granted, I promise a faithful compliance with the By-Laws of this Grange
and the Constitution and Laws of the State and National Granges.

    I have not previously applied for membership in this or any other jurisdiction.

.... 190 ....

Recommended by

Deposit, $ ....

Membership Application. *Source: author's personal collection.*

entrenched after the Civil War. Agricultural economy differed before and after the war. "Agriculture before the War Between the States had been largely self-sufficient. Food, clothing, and practically all necessities of life were obtained from the farm or by simple barter. Money was not needed for most purposes, and the majority of farmers were not dependent upon distant markets for their produce."[15]

Through organizing alliances, the farmers could benefit economically after the war. "Farmers could pool capital to buy seed, fertilizer, and equipment at reduced prices. They could market produce through cooperatives at higher prices than as individual sellers, and might also break monopolies in ginning, retailing, processing, and transportation."[16] This was a noble goal to be sure.

In spite of increased productivity, and perhaps because of it,

---

[15] Greer 62   [16] W.H. Morgan

the role of the individual farmer was to change drastically. "The agricultural decline of the late 1880's swept away thousand of optimistic, marginal farmers. The stubborn, genuine farmers remained; ready to demand political solutions for economic problems."[17] The Order of the Patrons of Husbandry or Grange was ready to help ease the farm family through the changes to come.

Agricultural communities were the bedrock of life in America prior to the Civil War. The same causes that gave rise to rural community development ushered in a vehicle for dispersion of information and education throughout the United States after the American Civil War. This was a pivotal period in the United Sates. So pervasive was the change and so quickly did it occur, it appears that those who were living through these changes did not recognize their enormous impact.

There were multiple forces in the last quarter of the nineteenth century of America including industrialization, expansion of cities, large-scale immigration and agricultural machinery. C. W. King described the motives for the large number of social movements in the post-war era: "But a spectacular abundance of social movements marks the society whose traditions have been shaken by industrial urbanism and whose structure is scarred by cleavages between diverse groups."[18]

The Grangers were noted in a study of such rural social movements describing the ideological motivations of the organization. Through politicizing the agrarian community, "The Grange originated as a radical organization based on the evolving ideology that combined elements of Jeffersonian

---

[17] W.H. Morgan   [18] King 13

Republicans with the aggressive liberalism of the Jacksonian period and a new desire to contain individual liberty through legislative controls on monopoly capitalism."[19]   Economic concerns were at the heart of the problem. "The republicans viewed capitalism as a relatively new form of tyranny that led to an oppressed laboring class."[20]   Still others comment on this element of the Grange motives, including these notes: "Knights of the Plow demonstrated the genesis of the cooperative concept in the mind of Oliver Kelley, and its priority within the Grange's early program."[21]

Book knowledge was suspect by farmers who eschewed the enterprise. The founding father of the Patron's of Husbandry recognized this challenge early on and Kelley "knew full well the narrow horizons of most farmers, their suspicion of those they considered to be strangers, and their disdain for new ideas."[22]   Kelley held out hope for the training of the farmer, however. "Kelley was convinced that technology coupled with broader knowledge about agriculture could transform farming from an occupation of drudgery and low cultural esteem into a profitable and dignified career."[23]

Kelley could empathize with the suspicion and frustration of the farmer. He tried working for the newly-formed Department of Agriculture, which was formed in 1862.[24] Kelley anticipated what later became the Farmers Institutes and the Department of Agriculture's extension service when he recommended that the department send agricultural lecturers into rural areas to impart new information with the intention of educating farmers

---

[19] T.A. Woods xv

[20] T.A. Woods 5

[21] Prescott 378

[22] Nordin, *Rich Harvest: A History of the Grange* 7

[23] T.A. Woods 27

[24] T.A. Woods 85

to help themselves.[25] Increasingly impatient with the slow dissemination of information emerging from the Department of Agriculture, he moved to a new appointment within the Post Office Department. During that time, the Grange began to take shape. A farmer during the era described his frustration with the arrogant approach to disseminating information. Dudley W. Addams provided this view in 1872:

> But, when the tillers of the soil have met in an agricultural society of any kind, it has been usually customary to select a lawyer, doctor, editor, or politician to tell us what he knows about farming. The idea has very rarely occurred to the managers of such institutions that it might be possible for a farmer to have anything to say on such occasions which should be either appropriate, interesting, or instructive. [26]

It is as though Patron founder, Kelley, exemplified the altruistic nature of a leader who seeks neither power nor acclaim, "perhaps securing their greatest satisfaction from a sheer sense of accomplishment."[27] Whatever the motive, it was to have a long-lasting effect on those who sought to carry on the mission for Kelley. The notion of shared control over the organization is further noted. "Very early in its career, effective control moved from the hands of original top officeholders out to the grass-roots functionaries."[28] This suggested that the aims of the order shifted over time, moving "from fraternal and educational to economic objectives"[29] and back again to its

---

[25] T.A. Woods 87
[26] Carstensen 27
[27] King 34
[28] King 113
[29] King 113

Loggers hauling trees pulled by horses.
Source: courtesy of Manistee County Historical Museum

original goals.

Grangers have been described as people who were "united in pride of their occupation and in their endorsements of the radical Grange platform.... The gathered farmers listened to orators pummel railroads, tariffs, and dishonest politicians."[30] All the flag waving at Fourth of July picnics did not lead to continuous harmony, however, for the larger battles were yet ahead for the farmers.

"By the end of 1873, Grange members had become confused about the goals and methods of the order." Problems arose when policies were unclear and lacked a national directive. The repercussion of this inaction has been described as neglecting to clearly distinguish between constitutional and unconstitutional political and religious discussion at Grange meetings."[31]

Aside from the political uncertainty and schism within the organization, the Grange continued to provide a positive outlet for rural social and educational involvement. The local experience has been described: "For many Grange members, subordinate grange meetings, with their emphasis on fellowship, ritual, and discussion of agricultural practices, formed the core of their Grange experience."[32]

Local Grange activities continued in spite of the decline in the national organization. *The Nation*, an 1876 publication, accused the organization of communistic leanings in this

---

[30] T.A. Woods 154
[31] T.A. Woods 163
[32] T.A. Woods 165

comment about the decline of the Grange:

> When the Grangers had once proclaimed that their object was to "fix rates," or, in other words, to declare by law what proportion of the market value of services they themselves should pay, and that they would not be bound by the terms of their contracts, it was perfectly clear that the Granger movement was rank communism, and its success in this country was against all reason and experience.[33]

There were other reasons for the unraveling of the Grange. "In 1875 Grange membership began to plummet as disappointed farmers deserted the Grange to search for new outlets for their protests against the merging system of monopoly capitalism."[34] In some circles, the Grange may have been unraveling, but in other circles the blueprint was embraced and followed, and the social order for the good of all was solace for the often isolated farm family.

Still others point to another motive occurring in the Grange to accommodate a shift in direction. "The Grange affords an interesting case of movement which, in its stable phase, returned to some of the original goals it discarded during the process of organization; at the same time the militancy and radicalism of its organizational phase was sloughed off, and—apart from agricultural problems—the movement in recent decades has generally favored the status quo."[35]

Short shrift is given for the Granger Movement with this explanation of faint praise. "Few movements ever become a

---

[33] Richards 58

[34] T.A. Woods 207

[35] Kelly 47

truly integrated part of a society although many are introduced as innovations."[36] The cultural drift described exemplifies the possible reasons for the demise of the Grange. "A resistance to or acceptance of a new proposal may hinge largely on these pre-existing tendencies toward change rather than one long-established tradition."[37]

Whitehead, Lecturer of the National Grange Education, reported in 1888 on some of the positive contributions of the Grange for farmers: "More than all other causes combined, the Grange secured the passage of National and State oleomargarine laws. It has secured Agricultural Experiments Stations for each state in the Union, The Inter-state Commerce Law. It is advocating pure food laws, equal taxation, control of corporations, checking 'trusts' and comers."[38]

After the Civil War, a quite different picture emerges for the economic forecast for the agricultural community. "Even if northern farmers had wanted to become commercially oriented capitalist producers, their possibilities were limited by generally poor access to markets, primitive agricultural technology, and a significant lack of technical agricultural knowledge on which to base new practices that would increase agricultural output."[39]

Not only were the farmers concerned over the problems noted above, but they were also feeling exploited by the middlemen in the process of bringing goods to the market. The effective squeeze felt by the farmers was described as follows:

> Thus the farmer is being told, on the one hand, that his interest lies with capital in combating the exorbitant wages of labor; and on the other hand, that his interest

---

[36] King 57
[37] King 88

[38] Whitehead 8
[39] T.A. Woods 16

lies with labor in combating the extortions of the middlemen. There are some indications that he is believing both.[40]

The farmers continued to be pitted against adversaries and their response was a mobilization that brought the dispersed farm families together for mutual support. Organization and action was a response to their plight. The result of these migrations or social-mobilization are noted: "The system development or crises theory was a product of this effort at placing the political system in its environmental and historical context."[41] Additional explanations for political participation were noted in a theory of empathy.

As people were mobilized from their rural, traditional, relatively static settings to the dynamic industrial, literate, media-saturated urban environment, they had an increased capacity to identify with others, to imagine themselves improving their social statuses, and mastering their environments.[42] Affiliations with organizations for mutual support were not at all uncommon in the rural community.

Work for the Ohio Agricultural Experiment Station in conjunction with The Ohio State University provides a picture of the participation by farm families in many social and educational activities. A study of 610 farm families gave evidence to multiple memberships in several fraternal organizations. Among the organizations noted by Tetreau were Woodman, Eagles, Elks, Moose, Knights of Columbus, Odd Fellows, Redman, and Masons. In addition to the lodges, membership and participation was studied in the Grange, Farm

---

[40] Rice 91
[41] Almond 8
[42] Almond 9

Bureau, Four-H Clubs, schools and churches. "Of the total group, 3 8 per cent [sic] of the families have memberships in the Grange or Farm Bureau or both."[43]

Events for the northern farmer proved to auger well for development through publications specific to their needs. "Since agricultural colleges and extension agencies were basically nonexistent at this time, agricultural editors and contributors were the only acknowledged experts on agricultural matters."[44] Oliver Hudson Kelley along with six other men, after experimenting with several farm organizational enterprises, established the Patrons of Husbandry. "Agricultural societies were designed to do many of the same things the agricultural press did, but they served as the palpable and immediate arm of agricultural innovation."[45]

Growing up a Granger was a natural event for Dora, as she had been called from a very young age. She and her siblings were taken as small children to the family-oriented activities that occurred at the local Grange. Dora was a life-long Granger. The lessons learned at the Grange Hall concerning a wide range of topics including the history of the Grange would eventually become incorporated into the plays and songs that she wrote for the Grange.

---

[43] Tetreau 5
[44] T.A. Woods 19
[45] T.A. Woods 20

2

Education and Family Life
1888-1901

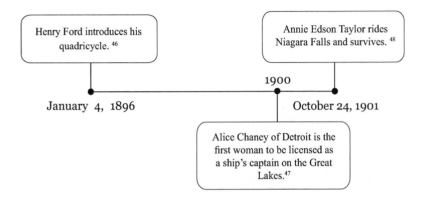

Henry Ford introduces his quadricycle. [46]

Annie Edson Taylor rides Niagara Falls and survives. [48]

1900

January 4, 1896

October 24, 1901

Alice Chaney of Detroit is the first woman to be licensed as a ship's captain on the Great Lakes.[47]

Stockman's path changed dramatically. Several lifelong influences were established during these years. Participating in the activities of the local Grange, Dora understood well the ritual and its appreciation for the richness of agricultural community. However, not all agreed with the delight of understanding history through ritual, and Grange detractors attempted to make the case for non-participation. Participation in the Temperance Movement was another guiding principle in her life. Education was enriched by attendance and graduation from Benzonia Academy. The cultural outposts gave rise to further study. The rural life was about to alter further through marriage, immediate motherhood, and a change of venue.

---

[46] *This Date in Michigan History*
[47] *This Date in Michigan History*

[48] *Chronology of Michigan Women's History*

Grange Ritual

It should be noted that the Grange is akin to other fraternal organizations and contains secret rituals that take place at each meeting. By 1899, the city of nearby Manistee hosted several fraternal groups described as "Lodges and Secret Societies." The history of Manistee notes their presence and contributions to the community: "Manistee has her full share of fraternal and benevolent societies, and almost every national lodge or organization of note is represented by a local chapter."[49] These organizations had their individual rituals and titles corresponding to the purpose of the group.

Likewise, membership in the Grange included an opportunity to move through the degrees that are adapted from early agricultural myths and traditions. Its founding father, Oliver Hudson Kelley, seemed to have found this particular aspect appealing.

Kelley suggested that a secret order with degrees and passwords devoted solely to the interest of farmers could revolutionize the farmers' profession. Degree lectures and

symbols could contain both practical agricultural and moral lessons. Kelley was convinced that the element of secrecy and the opportunity to gain new degrees would inspire continued interest. [50]

And thus began the Grange ritual which

Train. *Source: Manistee County Historical Museum*

---

[49] *The Salt City of the Inland Seas*

[50] T.A. Woods 94–95

featured elements from other popular fraternal organizations of the day, with added agricultural elements. The symbolism of the Grange incorporated agrarian themes that hearkened back to the earliest civilizations.

Grange Ritualism				
First Degree	Faith	Spring	Laborer	Maid
Second	Hope	Summer	Cultivator	Shepherdess
Third	Charity	Autumn	Harvester	Gleaner
Fourth	Fidelity	Winter	Husbandman	Matron

The higher degrees, Fifth, Sixth, and Seventh, are degrees of Pomona, Flora, and Ceres or Demeter and are conferred by Pomona Granges which are normally county Granges or District Granges depending upon the state: by the State Granges for the degree of Flora; by the National Grange in annual session of the Assembly of Demeter, in the case of the degree of Ceres.

These degrees are available to all those who fully subscribe to the long-established custom of teaching by symbols and emblems, to the principle of using the power of ritualism to bring out the finer characteristics of the members and the beauty of rural life. [51]

Such rituals were located in a small handbook entitled *Manual of Subordinate Granges of The Patrons of Husbandry* published in 1908. Adopted and issued by the National Grange, this book was in its ninth edition. It provided a floor plan of

---

[51] Robinson

seating arrangements for members and officers of the Grange along with the listing of degrees and the appropriate costume for each member to wear. An instructive example is the Degree of Shepherdess which is described in great detail including (as the book refers to it), "paraphernalia for the degree."

1. Pink veils to adorn the candidates in preparation room (1 ½ yards of Pink Illusion or some other fine transparent material.)

2. Roses (real or artificial) on desk of Overseer, to present to the Candidate.[52]

Degree Work

The symbolism of this Degree is the same as that of the Cultivator, and the work is readily understood by the manual. The candidates in this Degree are adorned in the preparation room with pink veils.

The O. should be prepared, at his desk, to present each candidate a rose, to be laid on the open Bible....[53]

The Order of Business for Regular Meeting in Fourth Degree were as follows:

1. Opening the Grange.
2. Reading the minutes of last meeting.
3. Reports of Committee on Candidates.
4. Balloting for candidates.
5. Proposals for membership.
6. Reports of standing committees.
7. Reports of special committees.

---

[52] *Manual of Subordinate Patrons of Husbandry 9th Edition*

[53] *Manual of Subordinate Patrons of Husbandry 9th Edition*

8. Bills and accounts.
9. Unfinished business.
10. Communications from the State or National Grange.
11. Have the reports to the County and State Granges been duly and promptly made?
12. New business.
13. Conferring degrees.
14. Literary programme.
15. Suggestions for the good of the Order.
16. Is any member sick or in distress?
17. Reading arid adopting minutes.
18. Closing.[54]

The opening of the Grange included a call to order as follows:

The hour of labor has arrived and the work of another day demands our attention. Let each repair to his or her allotted station.

Worthy Overseer, are all present correct?

Worthy Steward, you will ascertain. My assistants will make examination and report.

Worthy Master, we find all present correct.

Worthy Steward, are the gates properly guarded?

---

[54] *Manual of Subordinate Patrons of Husbandry 9th Edition*

They are, Worthy Master.
Worthy Steward, inform the Gate Keeper that we are
preparing for work. [55]

This ritual continued on and included a prayer and a song which was then followed by the balance of the order of business. The book continued with a listing of the different degree requirements and the appropriate passages to be recited. The section on staging of the programs was of particular interest and includes the guide for hiring of a "stage fitter who would be glad to take the contract to put in the slides and scenery similar to those used in opera houses."[56] The manual is quite clear on acquiring scenery that would reflect the four seasons of the year.

Grange Detractors

Not everyone was enamored with the Patrons of Husbandry. Local churches, feeling threatened by the competition for time and money of its members, often fought against the Grange, using the weapon of diatribes against its agrarian ritual. The immigrant Church and the views of the National Christian Association were negative towards the Patrons of Husbandry for a variety of reasons.

The National Christian Association also contended that the Grange interfered with the Church, since church members who were Grangers owed obligations to two organizations,

Grange Flag.
Source: Author's
personal collection.

---

[55] *Manual of Subordinate Patrons of Husbandry 9th Edition*

[56] *Manual of Subordinate Patrons of Husbandry 9th Edition 115*

and this meant a loss of interest in the Church. The dues paid to the Grange might have gone to the Church. The oath required by the Grange was regarded by the Church as one of infidelity, defeating justice, and the charity of the Patrons of Husbandry was looked upon as fictitious.[57]

There was a degree of incredulity by Grange members to these perceived barriers to joining. Even today some churches do not permit their members to belong to the Grange. This is difficult for Grange members to understand because of the strong religious nature of the Order. Most of the secrets of the Grange, like the secrets of living, are acquired with learning and experience. [58]

Another detractor attempts to make a case for avoiding the Grange. The notion of the benign farmer participating in the rights of the local Grange continues to this day. The symbols continue to be a subject of derision by those who object to the heathen influence. A more contemporary detractor has spoken out against the rituals of the Grange. The delivery is a collective diatribe against members of fraternities, such as the Masons in general and the Grange in particular, whom he identifies as the followers of Demeter and Ceres:

> Just as the Masons, the typical Grange member is probably involved in an organization about which he knows little. Many would be astonished at the origins of their organizations.... However, the Grange member— innocently or not—is in an organization *which is steeped in an evil as ancient as the Lodge!* It doesn't matter whether or not the Grange actually practices paganism, occultism, or human sacrifice. What matters is that

---

[57] O. Fritiof Ander 161   [58] Trump 6

it has chosen to wrap itself in a panoply of symbolism right out of the pit of hell.[59]

Clearly an alternate point of view on the bucolic country life, the Grange songbooks included hymns and praise for the abundance of life given by a living and merciful God.

Cultural Outposts

The symbolic use of shafts of wheat is described in a more positive manner by others. The shafts of wheat are prominent on the emblem for the Grange. "Prominently featured in Grange ritualism is the cornucopia, the Horn of Plenty, in which the earnest Patron voices his faith in God as the Great Provider, and acknowledges his own responsibility for cooperation with both Nature and the Almighty."[60] The more generous commentator continues with an explanation of the cornucopia:

The cornucopia emblem is designed to teach the lesson that we are to dispense as well as to accumulate; not to gather simply for the sake of possession, but that out of such plentiful stores as diligent labor has produced others may derive enjoyment in the sharing of the abundant gifts of harvest. There is always the reminder of stores laid up against the day of possible want, and so the Horn of Plenty in the Grange, filled by the zealous toil of many brothers and sisters, will be ready with its overflowings of knowledge, wisdom, goodness and abundance to supply whatever wants the future may bring.[61]

---

[59] Schnoebelen

[60] Gardner 342

[61] *Manual of Subordinate Granges of the Patrons of Husbandry*

The harvest included education and entertainment for the agricultural community. For the lonely women living life upon the farm, the Patrons of Husbandry must have seemed like a godsend and almost too good to be true. Future setbacks aside, for the Grange, there were some gains. The benefit of training could be long-lasting. "Their importance lies in the changes they made or failed to make in the larger society than in the experience and training they gave their members. Communes eased the pain of...the loneliness of youth, and most...provided satisfying work and companionship."[62]

Popular culture for the farm family could be shared at the farm family fraternity. The Patrons of Husbandry, or Grange, with its meeting halls and featured speakers, was the local cultural outpost. The role of women in the United States was changing during the period from roughly 1865 to 1925. Expectations and opportunities for women were expanding, and education was seen as a vital link to help with the development of children. The family remained at the heart of the enterprise.

Expectations for women between 1890 and 1950 in America have been described in a broader perspective than had previously been the case. They were "expected to be guardians of culture, charged with moral, intellectual and physical upbringing of the children."[63] The increased horizons for women brought a new outlook and a new challenge for the agrarian woman, while the larger communities had ladies' literary clubs providing opportunity for

Young Dora portrait on tin.
Source: Stockman Family Archives

---

[62] Taylor and Case 9   [63] Lynes 3

study in cities and small towns and the Lyceum resumed activity after the Civil War. "It was the Chautauqua that was, in a very real sense, the progenitor of what might be called the mass middlebrow audience for culture in America."[64] In addition to seeking self-improvement through the Chautauqua, Americans "... heard lectures, attended the theater, went to curiosity museums and circuses" during the Gilded Age.[65]

Dora Hall represented the new type of female agrarian ambition. By the time Dora was fourteen, she sat for the teacher's examination and was approached by a local newspaper publisher to write for the Bear Lake Beacon. Early education had been conducted locally.

Education prior to college was limited initially to the very basic necessities for farm children. "But, later, many yeomen [farmers] who belonged to the organization recognized that an education could be of value to agrarian youths, provided that it was tailored to their needs."[66] The traditional pattern of school participation by rural families was discovered through studying the attendance patterns of several Ohio counties in the late twenties. "The age of 14 is considered as normal for eighth grade completion." It is noteworthy too, "that 90 percent of the children (6–14) are normal or advanced as to school grade attained."[67]

For the Grangers, however, much more was expected. "Since education was the fundamental objective for which the Grange was founded, it is not surprising to find that the order sought educational improvements at all levels that could possibly benefit members and their families."[68]

---

[64] *Manual of Subordinate Granges of the Patrons of Husbandry*
[65] Roberts
[66] Nordin 58
[67] Tetreau 18
[68] Nordin 6

Dora Hall was about to take on an added dimension with attendance at a religious revival meeting. She would become a representative of the modem agrarian progressive woman through marriage, motherhood, education, and continued involvement with the Grange. "By the end of the nineteenth century, American newspapers and magazines brimmed with speculation about the crisis of marriage and the family. Four developments gave rise to a steadily growing alarm: the rising divorce rate, the falling birthrate among 'the better sort of people,' the changing position of women, and the so-called 'revolution in morals.'"[69] A woman could become useful and at the same time continue to study, it seemed, if there was a direct benefit to the immediate family. Dora was about to demonstrate the art of the possible.

Temperance

Religious life in Manistee County included the presence of a large Union Hall for the Women's Christian Temperance Union, according to *The Manistee Daily News*. Abuse of alcohol was a real problem facing the family. A colorful summary of temperance activity in Manistee at the turn of the century is noteworthy.

In 1874, we passed through a siege known as the temperance war, and for all that the cause met with great opposition the largest auditorium in the city (the old Congregational church) was densely crowded for thirty-five successive evenings with people who listened with the deepest interest to lectures and enthusiastic

---

[69] Larch 83

speeches, and more than 2,000 persons signed the pledge. Those who opposed the cussed, as is always the case, resorted to many petty meannesses such as girdling trees, killing horses, injuring property in various ways, and even threatening life. Enthusiasm in the temperance crusade ran to such a height that the ladies of the city determined to establish a reading room on River Street, which they hoped might attract many who had heretofore been accustomed to spend their leisure hours in the saloons. The result was the building of Temperance Hall (now Olympian Club), which was erected in 1874-75, and paid for by the efforts of the women of Manistee.[70]

Future legislator, Dora, was born only two years after the start of the temperance movement. Stockman would eventually become an ardent spokesperson for the cause of temperance. She actively prepared herself for this role through study and application. The Grange actively supported the goals of leading a temperate life. The temperate life included a prohibition against the use of tobacco too. Lyrics written by Dora Stockman in *Banish Tyrant Cigaret* to the tune of *Yankee Doodle* describes the problems of cigarettes in society.

The children of America, Their friends and dear
  relation,
Have started war on Cigaret To drive him from the nation.

(Chorus)
Down with Cigaret, we shout, We pledge we will not

---

[70] *The Salt City of the Inland Seas*

smoke, sir
As knights of old, we're fighting bold, From our land
he must go, sir.

We want pure air to help us grow, We hate the poison
smoke, sir.
We want clear heads to win life's race, No nicotine for
us, sir.

(Chorus)
We will not waste a single dime, We'll put them into
homes, sir,
In autos and in aeroplanes, They'll give us lots more
fun, sir.

(Chorus)
They cannot fool us with their talk, Or billboard
advertising,
The radio ads we'll all turn off, Kind friends we are
advising.

(Chorus)
We ask you folks who make the weed, to change your
farms and factories.
Grow sugar plums, and Christmas trees, They're much
more to our liking.

(Chorus)
The tyrant Cigaret is bold, He is a billionaire sir,
But Freedom claims, From our land he must go, sir.

27

(Chorus)
Down with Cigaret, we shout, We pledge we will
    not smoke, sir
As knights of old, we're fighting bold, From our land
    he must go, sir.[71]

Marriage

With a strong interest in religious participation through, Church, Grange and the temperance movement, it was, therefore, not out of character that Dora Stockman would meet her future husband at a religious event. Religious Revival Meetings were common fair in both the city and in country life in 1888. At the age of sixteen, Dora Hall met a widower from the nearby community of Pleasanton at a religious revival meeting.[72]

Francis Stockman was raising two young boys and living with his widowed mother, Elizabeth. The marriage license supplied the particulars of the bride and groom. "1889 Marriage license 397, Florence [sic] M. Stockman, age 34 of Pleasanton to Endo[sic] L. Hall, age 17 of Marilla." The *Manistee Democrat,* a local newspaper, described the occasion of their marriage on August 9, 1889, under "Yates Items." She is photographed in her wedding dress.

Married at the residence of the bride's parents (Mr. and Mrs. L. F. Hall), Francis Stockman of Pleasanton and Eudora Hall of Marilla; Rev R. A. Shaw of Fern, Mason County officiating. About one hundred guests were invited, but owing to sickness and the rain, a

---

[71] Michigan State Grange Song Collection   [72] D. Stockman, *The Story of Myself*

number were unable to attend. Friends were present from Pleasanton, Bear Lake, Manistee, and about sixty from Clion and Marilla. The presents were numerous, valuable and useful. The happy couple repair to his farm and enter upon the realities of married life.[73]

Realities set in quickly with instant motherhood and a mother-in-law. She describes marriage, motherhood, disease, and health problems common during the era. In 1890, her older step-son died of malignant diphtheria. The following year, 1891, her mother-in-law, Elizabeth Stockman died.[74]

Agrarian women became brides as a useful helpmate for the farmer. Marriage to a man seventeen years her senior with a ready-made family must surely have been a challenge for Dora. A more optimistic view would place the woman on the farm as an opportunity to build a life that was desirable over other options. "A marriage was an economic relationship, and wives acknowledged their duty to accept the lives their husbands provided. The economic reciprocity entailed in a marriage varied according to class."[75] Others suggested that the reason for farmers to marry was for economic gain. "The farmer confronted himself with the many tasks which usually fall to the share of women-folk on a farmstead, and is frequently in a position where he cannot afford not to marry if an opportunity

Dora, Francis, Marian, and Curtis Stockman.
Source: Stockman Family Archives

---

[73] *The Manistee Democrat*
[74] D. Stockman, *The Story of*

[75] Fink, *Agrarian Women: Wives and Mothers in Rural Nebraska* 67

arises."[76]

A Change of Venue

The young family struck out on a new adventure in nearby Arcadia, Michigan. Dora's autobiography indicates that the bride and groom began farming, but seemed quickly disillusioned and sold their farm in 1891 and began a mercantile business in Arcadia. Her unpublished autobiography creates a colorful picture of the rugged Michigan life and the continuing problems with farming. "Because of hard farm conditions, drought and low prices, in 1891 we sold the farm and went into a mercantile business in Arcadia, where we shipped produce for farmers on a small commission." Her autobiography tells of personal challenges:

In the meantime, I had bad health owing to typhoid fever, the grippe, and the strain of maternity, weighing only 65 pounds. I was sent to Ann Arbor. A very skillful doctor told me to do three things if I want to live and be well: 'To eat the things I ought to eat,' To help me do this, he gave me a government bulletin; 'To exercise outdoors,' To help me do this, he gave me a government bulletin; 'To forget how badly I felt.'[77]

She clearly found the strength to move forward with great zeal. Her recovery and energy led to further education and outside interests as noted in her autobiography. "I took a correspondence Domestic-Science course and a Moody Bible Institute course and wrote for newspapers...meanwhile being

---

[76] Rice 123

[77] D. Stockman, *The Story of Myself*

housekeeper, mother and clerking in our store."[78]

While many could take advantage of college, there were those who could not find training in alternative programs. One such program has been described at the University of Wyoming. When the university opened in 1886, the student profile included a high percentage of adult students. "As a first step towards meeting the needs of those students who were unable to come to the campus, the University encouraged the public to establish local extension centers."[79] Clearly, the nation was interested in creating a positive educational atmosphere near home and also out on the range.

Alternative education in the form of correspondence courses had an early beginning with the opportunity for students of the Bible to study while at home. What was no longer a novelty at the end of the twentieth century must have been quite adventurous at the end of the nineteenth century. Nonetheless, Dora embraced this chance for further education.

Biblical Studies

The program started by Dwight L. Moody found a wide audience. "During the second half of the nineteenth century no evangelist was better known than Dwight Lyman Moody (1837-1899). The achievements of his life fulfilled in many ways the aspirations of a wide spectrum of American believers."[80] Evangelizing using a simple and clear message quickly captured the imagination of many Americans. "Moody presented a basic Christian message, which he summarized as the 'Three R's':

---

[78] D. Stockman, *The Story of Myself*
[79] Nel 97
[80] Noll 288

Ruin by Sin, Redemption by Christ, and Regeneration by the Holy Ghost. He did not expound learned theology, nor did he promote sophisticated formulas for Christian action in society."[81] It was a practical approach that appealed to many. It offered a chance for education through the center started in Chicago for lay workers.

"Moody's personal influence was extended through the important institutions he founded. These included a Bible training center for lay workers in Chicago (later the Moody Bible Institute)...."[82] Moody himself had credibility, both in the U.S. and Great Britain, and he had the financial support of a core of well-to-do Chicago businessmen.

> The Institute's ministries extended beyond the training school. Many people came to know it for its publishing efforts through Moody Press and Moody Monthly. It has been a forerunner in religious radio and in producing films that integrate science and Scripture. Furthermore, its history reveals an innovative institution in the areas of curriculum development, including day-school, evening-school and correspondence-school programs and a specialized program for preparing missionary aviation pilots.[83]

Clearly, Dora applied herself through the Moody program, resulting in a published thesis. A note that her thesis on *The Present Day Influence of the Life of Christ* was later put into book form by the American SS Mission and called *A Bountiful Harvest* was discovered in her autobiography. During this period, Dora

---

[81] Noll 289
[82] Noll 290

[83] Reid 67

Stockman gave birth to her first child—a son, Lee, in January of 1892.

Benzonia Academy

The Moody program must certainly have influenced her move and solidified her views on temperance. The family became disillusioned with the somewhat wild community of Arcadia with, as Dora described it: "A saloon and two blind pigs, together with a German beer garden decided us to move to Benzonia, in 1895, which was then the home of a Congregational College."[84] The move to Benzonia was fortunate in many ways for the Stockmans. Dora began clerking once again in the shop while further education was close at hand. The location of their business in Benzonia remains and is now used as a pottery shop. They bought timberland and ran some logging camps while in Benzonia.

In summer and midwinter, she began work in Benzonia College then on the Teachers State Certificate List. Stockman, a married woman, began classes at the Academy in 1895. The program notes from the First Grand Concert by the Benzonia College Choral Society, at Case's Music hall, on Tuesday evening, November

First Congregational Church Choir. *Source: Benzie Area Historical Museum, Benzonia, Michigan*

---

[84] D. Stockman, *The Story of Myself*

26th at 8:15 included several married women in the program including Mrs. F. M. Stockman as one of six contraltos. She graduated in 1899 from Benzonia College but continued her studies until 1902. The title of the institution had undergone a few changes as the community changed. In 1897, *The Benzonia Register* lists graduates of Benzonia College and Prepatory Departments as compiled from various dates. 1897 Prep. Dept. Mrs. Dora Hall Stockman [penciled in "Lansing, Mich, RFD"]. Also penciled in the college registry was a note on "Willis A. Benton (B.L.)," her sister Phebe J. Hall-Benton's husband in attendance at the academy. It was becoming a family tradition, with the addition of Dora's brother. The college register noted Dora's brother also in attendance at Benzonia. Welcome F. Hall joined his sister in 1900 at the academy.[85]

Benzonia, Michigan, was on the map then and continues to be famous for the historical writer, Bruce Catton. Catton chronicled his boyhood in Benzonia and life at the Benzonia Academy:

> The country was laced with railroads, the big cities like Chicago and Detroit were within easy reach, and the colleges that had been brought into being took root and prospered. There were Adrian, Alma, Hillsdale, Olivet, Kalamazoo, Hope, the state university at Ann Arbor, the agricultural college at East Lansing, and a number of state-supported normal colleges to train teachers. They grew up with a growing country. But the country around Benzonia College never grew up. It passed from lusty adolescence to an uneasy senility. When the lumber was gone...there was nothing much to take its place.[86]

---

[85] *The Manistee County Directory*　　　　　　[86] Catton 32

Dora notes her academic work at the Academy, "I finished required work for a literary course and also a Master's Degree."[87] Academic work was not Dora's only focus of attention. On June 20, 1900 at 2:30 p.m., she performed an alto solo singing *Where Did You Come From, Baby Dear* by Neidlinger and *Cradle Song,* and again in 1902, she sang *Voices of Angels* by Wilson. She was also a church soloist. The museum of the academy houses a church yearbook with Dora pictured in the front row to the right of center. The choir notes from the First Congregational Church listed her voice as contralto.

While Dora continued to write, work in the family business, and attend school, there was still an unfulfilled ambition in an even greater challenge. Dora and her husband had a motto that guided their lives and that was to make their little corner of the world better than when they found it. It would not be long before her little corner became a state.

---

[87] D. Stockman, *The Story of Myself*

3

Grange Writer on the Move
1902-1909

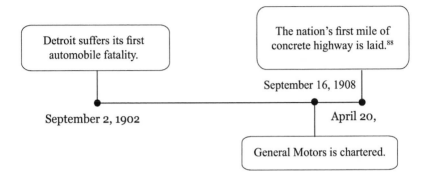

Detroit suffers its first automobile fatality.

The nation's first mile of concrete highway is laid.[88]

September 16, 1908

September 2, 1902

April 20,

General Motors is chartered.

Motivation and increased educational opportunity for service beyond the local community resulted from a change in personal circumstances for the Stockman family. Towards the close of the decade, Dora enlarged the scope of her experience through writing and lecturing for the Grange. With the support of her husband, she became a model of the modern woman.

Domestic Realities

Noble goals were not all that was required of these entrepreneurs, however. Township records note the value of the Stockman general store in comparison to another enterprise owned by Henry Starke. In 1895–96, the "Henry Starke General Store valued at $5,590." Frances [sic] Stockman General Store valued at $650.00."[89] Clearly, a change was forthcoming when,

---

[88] *This Date in Michigan History*   [89] *Manistee County Directory*

in the next year, the figures were even further apart. The records from Arcadia, Michigan showed the values of both the Starke and Stockman general stores in 1897–98: "Starke General Store valued at $2,165. Francis Stockman General Store valued at $100." This also marks the change in the physical health of Francis Stockman. According to family reports, Francis Stockman was advised to reduce his physical activity due to health problems. The young family had settled in a smaller community.

There were soon to be more exciting challenges awaiting Dora. She was typical of her era in some respects. "Two generations of middle-class American women from 1880 to the close of the 1920s were dominated by aspirations of a nature now quite alien. They desired a public life of restless activism, and saw fulfillment for these desires only in terms of extreme individualism."[90] Publications for the farm family included and supported the further independence for women. Agitation for full participation in the world was found in several contemporary journals during this period. Certainly it may be presumed that Dora was an avid reader. A typical issue of an agricultural journal discusses the arguments in favor of suffrage. The *Michigan Farmer and State Journal of Agriculture,* November 1, 1890, household supplement, received a response from a contributor to the previous edition letter concerning suffrage:

> One might as well argue that boys should not be allowed to vote upon attaining their majority on the plea that they will undoubtedly vote as their fathers do, as to say that women will do so. The great mass of American women today are thinking women, and while occasionally you

---

[90] Conway 217

find one of the "ivy-vine" type, the great majority can think for themselves, and if need be act for themselves too.

And suppose she did want office! Equal rights to male and female should be the cry of every woman, whether she wishes to avail herself of them or not. No, I am not a radical woman suffragist; do not belong to a "club;" Personally, I have my share of "rights." still I would like the privilege of voting if I want to; and I expect to have it too, someday. [91]

Though Stockman did not write this letter, the sentiments contained therein and the suggestion of a woman seeking office are prescient indeed. The right to vote would have to wait almost twenty years and, in the meantime, the education of women continued. While waiting for the vote, how would a women's education be used?

The functionalism of and education for women of that era and the resulting guilt if the education was not put to good use in the world have been and continue to be a topics for discussion. "The value of knowledge lay in its social utility to an era that accepted the Spencerian vision of society. This utilitarian notion of the education they had received added to the burden of guilt of post-Civil War American Women."[92]

While the home of rural women may have been the confines of the farm, they still found a wide variety of activities to engage their time. An acceptable political and economic role for women in rural America at the turn of the century has been described

---

[91] E. Woods   [92] Conway 248

with notable conditions: "A woman lost social favor by engaging in any economic or political activity outside the context of the family, but almost any degree of crossover into male roles was permissible if done within the family's system of control."[93] Women on the farm might have their own economic enterprise, which they operated individually, but the earnings would often be paid to husbands. "Achieving even limited parity on the farm depended on her husband's willingness to share more than on the woman's willingness to work."[94]

Clearly, Dora enjoyed the support from her somewhat older husband, for if she had not received such encouragement, it is unlikely that her actions would have taken her so far afield from home and hearth. Driven by the reported goals for women at the turn of the century, Dora found socially accepted ways to serve both her personal and professional ambitions, exceeding many woman of her era. "Early republican ideology had as one of its main tenets the proposition that women should become useful rather than ornamental."[95] Dora was to prove herself to be far from ornamental.

This usefulness is reflected in the types of literature available to women during this period. Beyond the agricultural journals, other works informed the world of women and increasingly gave rise to a more liberal perspective.

Against the prevailing view of the day in the later part of the nineteenth century, the material described the reality of fiction reading by women. "Polemic against the common expectation that women automatically and unreflectingly identified with central women characters, or that they would be unfailingly corrupted by reading about matters concerning sexuality, was

---

[93] Fink, *Open Country Iowa: Rural Women. Tradition and Change*

[94] Franck and Brownstone

[95] Larch 82

met head-on within the pages of those very books which caused conservative commentators the greatest anxiety."[96] The built-in social contract has been described in sensational fiction.

Excitement, indeed, but not without its own self-imposed limitations. For other contemporary reviewers felt obliged to stress that however undesirable the subject-matter of the sensation novel might be, the resolution of its plot invariably supports prevalent social and moral values and formations.[97]

One of the motives for women reading was vicarious fellowship as noted by Larch: "Reading, in the Victorian and Edwardian period, as now, was an activity through which a woman could become aware of the simultaneity of the sensations of difference and of similarity; it allowed her to assert her sense of selfhood, and to know that she was not alone in doing so."[98] Not only was fiction a popular staple but also non-fiction provided another window on the world for women.

American critics of feminism preferred to base their case on the contention that a woman's usefulness to society and her own self-fulfilling work lay precisely in her sacred duties as wife and mother. The major premise of feminism—that women should be useful, not ornamental—had to be conceded, even while the conclusions feminists drew from this premise—the conclusions, they would have argued, that followed irresistibly—were vigorously repudiated.[99]

One vehicle for becoming less than ornamental was through a practical education related to the appropriate sphere

---

[96] K. Flint 255

[97] K. Flint 281

[98] K. Flint 329–330

[99] Larch 84–85

of women. However, the reality of economic necessity did not always afford attention to education. Work was a necessity for many. "In 1852 women composed 2/3–3/4 of factory employees, mostly in eastern mills, and at the lowest pay."[100] The following picture emerges of the change occurring for women in Western culture:

> In the mid-nineteenth century, defenders of the home had relied heavily on the appeals to woman's duty to sacrifice herself for the good of others, but by 1900 this kind of rhetoric, even when translated into the progressive jargon of "service," had begun to seem decidedly out-of-date. The view that woman lived best by living for others gradually gave way to the view that woman too had a right to self-fulfillment, a right, however, that could best be realized in the home. In a word, the critics of feminism began to argue that motherhood and housewifery themselves constituted satisfying "careers," which required special training in "homemaking," "domestic science," and "home economics."[101]

The invention of such terms expressed an attempt to dignify housework by raising it to the level of a profession. Dignified or not, the work had to be done and could be done efficiently and effectively through training, leaving more time for the work of educating and raising children. Dora, armed with her degree and experience as a writer, mother and wife, continued to work toward a greater purpose.

---

[100] Stock 185   [101] Larch 84–85

Beyond the Domestic Sphere

Rural women in particular faced a challenge. Women were active in the grassroots protest organizations. The Grange included women in its discussion groups and tried to draw them into a wider organizational circle than they had experienced on the family farm. Women were also writers and organizers in the Farmer's Alliance, which advocated woman suffrage as part of its program.[102]

The Grange writer, Stockman, was an active participant in the life of the Grange in Michigan. However, the strength of the Grange may have been diminished in some circles. The Grange provided Dora with an ideal platform for promoting progressive agrarian ideas of her day, leading from a log cabin birth to a position as an elected public official in Michigan. Stockman engaged in areas beyond the domestic sphere. She continued with the important work for the farm families.

Rural grassroots protests dissolved around the turn of the century while there was still much to be gained utilizing the forum of the Grange. "The farm economy was improving, siphoning off some of the discontent. Disagreements within the movements also left some people disenchanted and unwilling to make the economic and personal sacrifices necessary for continuing agitation."[103]

While Dora Stockman was well acquainted with domestic science, she had other callings that took her away from her own home and into the homes of farm families throughout the state. For some women, domestic spheres were eclipsed by interest in other activities.

---

[102] Larch 23

[103] Fink, *Agrarian Women: Wives and Mothers in Rural Nebraska* 24

43

"The entrance of women into teaching was slow."[104]   As the curriculum and years in high school expanded there was, however, an increased need for women to become teachers. "As local education costs rose in the 1870s and 1880s, communities that had previously preferred male teachers discovered that women, who earned about 60 percent of male salaries at best, were appropriate teachers for their children."[105]

This proved to be a double-edged sword, as some communities became suspicious of the expanded role afforded to women. The changing status of women struck the most casual observer as one of the most telling signs of the times. More and more women went to college, joined clubs and organizations of all kinds, and entered the labor force. Industry had invaded the family and stripped it of its productive functions. Work formerly carried on in the household could be carried out more efficiently in the factory. Even recreation and child-rearing were being taken over by outside agencies, the former by the dancehall and the popular theater, the latter by the school.[106]

Stockman did not view the programs at the local Grange Hall as taking away from the child's experience but, instead, saw it as enriching the entire family through the family-centered activities. The unique type of creative woman that Dora seemed to represent in her life's work is suggested in these remarks: "An emancipated woman thus does not necessarily accept comparison with more 'active' male proclivities as a measure of her equivalence, even after it has become quite clear that she can match man's performance and competence in most spheres of achievement. True equality can only mean the right to be uniquely creative."[107]

---

[104] Stock 188
[105] Stock 188–189

[106] Larch 84
[107] Erikson 26

Further Education

In April of 1902, Dora accompanied Francis on a move to Oregon. The trip was designed to aid her husband's health. He was suffering bronchial trouble, so a change of climate was undertaken. "My husband had such bad bronchial trouble that we sold and traded our property, store and sold some land and went West."[108] Dora, now age 30, returned to Michigan four months later in August to help her own ailing mother. Health problems aside, it appears as though her time was not at the sickbed only.

During her time apart from her husband, Dora continued her education. She began teaching and study at Hillsdale College in Hillsdale, Michigan, in 1902, while stepson Marion started Michigan State College (MSC). "I taught in the college and took work. I came out at the end of the year having paid my own and my young son's expenses with $50 left. I had a degree and a Teacher's State Certificate."[109]

In 1903, her husband returned to Michigan and purchased the Grand River View Farm outside of Lansing, Michigan. Four days were allotted for the celebration of accomplishments at the small privately-supported college. From June 14 to 18, 1903, Commencement Exercises were held at Hillsdale College in Hillsdale, Michigan. On Class Day Mrs. Dora H. Stockman of Lansing, Michigan, presented the class poem "Our Debt." The Class Roll notes major areas of study with the names of the graduating seniors. The largest grouping with ten students includes Stockman under the now arcane heading of "Normal." This was later referred to as a teaching degree or Life Teacher's

---

[108] D. Stockman, *The Story of Myself*   [109] D. Stockman, *The Story of Myself*

Hillsdale College Commencement Program. *Courtesy of Hillsdale College Archives, Michael Alex Mossey Library, Hillsdale College, Hillsdale, MI 49242*

Certificate, a Bachelor of Arts and Bachelor of Pedagogy. Dora Stockman was included in the Class Officers serving as Secretary. The graduation program from Hillsdale College notes her membership in the outstanding literary society (*Germanae Sodales*). It is interesting that, in the printed commencement program, the designation of a married woman was reserved only for Dora.[110]

Stockman suffered a personal loss in 1905. Her only daughter, Lucy, survived six days following her birth of complications from *Spina bifida*. In that same year, Dora's mother died. Lucy J. Hall was buried at the Marilla Cemetery in the Hall family plot.

Thus it was, in the following year, that Dora continued her pursuit of multiple activities, adding yet another new credit to

---

[110] Hillsdale College Commencement Excercises Program

her creative accomplishments. She sold her first story to the *Michigan Farmer* entitled "The Price of a Farm" in 1906.[111] The *Michigan Farmer* is a long running agricultural newspaper created in support of the causes of agriculture and more specifically the Patrons of Husbandry.

It was an ideal vehicle to promote the Grange activities, including the notices of forthcoming events and suggestions for meetings at the local Grange Hall. Dora was to have a long tenure with the publication ranging from writer, advertising agent and finally editor. By virtue of her long-term editorial stint with The *Michigan Patron* she became a member of the Michigan Women's Press Association.

Francis Stockman was a supportive husband, given the attitude of most farmers of the day. Following his health problems, he remained at home and supported Dora's travels in her work for the Grange. Dora Stockman described her husband in her autobiography:

> Mr. Stockman had but one year at College, but was a highly educated man, keeping up with the education of his family, and the latest religious and scientific thought. He was an industrious, thrifty worker with fine ideals; an affectionate husband and father, ready to sacrifice cheerfully for his family, with a strong attitude for education for himself and all his family.[112]

Health restored, Dora gave birth at age 35 to her second son, Verne, in 1907. It was not long, however, before Dora was on the move as a result of her debut on the lecture platforms of farm institutes in 1908. Dora was not the trailblazer in working

---

[111] D. Stockman, *The Story of Myself*   [112] D. Stockman , *The Story of Myself*

for the Grange; indeed, other women were forerunners in establishing the pattern that was followed by Dora. There were two such noteworthy Michigan Granger women before Stockman's entrance on the speakers' platform. Mary Anne Mayo characterizes the pioneering efforts of agrarian women leaders. She was, according to the Jennie Buell biography (1908), born in Michigan in 1845. She began teaching high school at 17 in Battle Creek, Michigan. Buell presents Mayo as a frequent Grange lecturer and organizer who traveled many miles to enhance the aims of the Grange.[113] Both Mary Anne Mayo and Jennie Buell made vital contributions to women in agriculture.

The Grange was unique from other fraternal organizations by including the family in all of its activities. How could women hope to maintain the family unit if the lure of the urban area drew young people from the farm to the city like a magnet? Indeed, it has been noted, "for a number of decades, a movement of young men and women from farms to industrial centers has been in progress."[114]

The Grange was both an inside and outside agency, providing an approved and endorsed family activity. The type of work in which the women of the Grange participated has been well established. The early setup of the Grange provided that four of the officers must always be women, thereby limiting the office eligibility of men. Another instance of woman's work in the Grange is found in the creation of degree teams, drill teams, tableau groups, choruses, and other working units which had proved invaluable Grange assets.[115]

---

[113] Fink, *Agrarian Women: Wives and Mothers in Rural*

[114] Rice 121 *Nebraska*

[115] Gardner, *The Grange— Friend of the Farmer 196*

However, Dora went beyond the pattern and created her own trail. Francis remained at home and supported Dora in her outreach to farm families. He supported her activities by caring for the boys, permitting her travels. Dora was not quite at home on the farm. In an interview with her son, Verne Stockman, another point of view emerged. The impression left on her young boy during her frequent absences was poignant. He recalled the many occasions of seeing his mother off at the railroad station or greeting her upon her return from her travels. Stockman's son commented on the family arrangements that permitted his mother's many absences.

Early on, her husband became the homebody and encouraged her to involve herself with the works outside of the home. Stockman was not enthusiastic about personal domestic arts, it seems, and, according to her son, it was mutually agreed that she should travel for her work with the Grange and later for the State of Michigan. [116] Could it be that Dora was not quite at home on the Grange?

She was a prolific writer and, according to her son, Verne, she would write on any material that was handy. Stockman, it is reported, took whatever time was available to write. On her first flight to Washington to attend a meeting, while men around her were evidently airsick, she wrote a poem. Scraps of paper and old notebooks became the beginning of her many literary creations. Stockman's writing chronicled the virtues of the rich life on the farm that was possible through full participation in the Grange. She characterized life upon the farm without the agency of the Grange as bleak without the assistance from this now almost-forgotten cooperative enterprise at the turn of the century in the midwestern state of Michigan.

---

[116] V. & L. Stockman

49

Though the Grange may have continued to fade from the landscape in some quarters, the seeds planted brought a rich harvest in educational enterprise that has survived in the land grant colleges throughout the United States in the twentieth century. That the enterprise remained successful is still debatable. A glimpse of the idealized past is possible through Dora's lens as a Grange playwright.

4

Setting the Stage
1910-1916

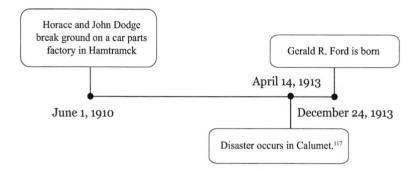

Horace and John Dodge break ground on a car parts factory in Hamtramck

Gerald R. Ford is born

April 14, 1913

June 1, 1910

December 24, 1913

Disaster occurs in Calumet.[117]

The social causes that gave rise to popular entertainments for American audiences were not limited to the city or town communities. Entertainments were also found at the local Grange Hall. Audience expectations are also discovered through a backward glance at the events of the era. As a grassroots writer, Stockman was reflecting the larger theatrical forum and social virtues in creating a variety of works for the Grange.

These presentations were useful for training and reflected the broad social agenda of the era. As a lecturer for the State Grange, Stockman was able to furnish a number of theatrical vehicles including pageants and dramas that advocated cultural assimilation through realistic presentations and themes noted in her plays. Understanding this type of play and its uses provides further appreciation of this multi-talented Grange writer.

---

[117] *Chronology of Michigan Women's History*

Grassroots Writer

Among the many and varied talents of Dora Stockman was her ability to create pageants, plays, poetry and songs for the Grange. She was an outstanding public speaker and prolific writer on contemporary themes of concern to her audience. During this phase of her life, she set a course that would eventually lead her further into the public arena and farther away from home.

Stockman's contribution to the Grange was not only for the adult audience as in *The Price of a Farm,* but she was to realize great acclaim with her work for the juvenile Grange. Juvenile Granges continue today but with a new title of 4-H. In 1910, H.R. Pattengill published a collection of plays written by Dora for young people entitled *Book of Dialogs.* The list of titles includes seasonal entries as well as clearly didactic pieces promoting modern science and agricultural technology such as *Dr. Mary's Prescription.*

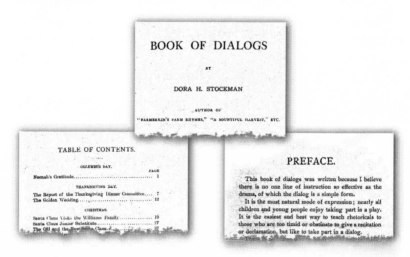

Book of Dialogs Source: *Michigan State University Archives and Historical Collections*

Pageants

Stockman also wrote and produced pageants, which saluted the Grange and its history. Pageants have been a popular community staple providing living reminders of past glories and struggles. A 1906 English journal article discussed the importance of pageantry in community life. Though the article focused on the heraldry of British royalty, the motive for pageantry has universal appeal.

"In any case, we believe, the spirit of mind which is stirred by the spectacle of great Royal pageantries is just that spirit which, if it is not allowed to develop into contemptuous pride, does tend to make and keep a nation great and happy." This journal article concludes with remarks that may be in keeping with Stockman's aims: "Men always dislike being warned of evil to come, but they are never made angry by being reminded of good that is past. It is the greatest of the provinces of pageantry that it reminds."[118]

Education occurred in many forms. Theater provides yet another example of a manner in which to educate and uplift while at the same time provide entertainment. In addition to creating plays and pageants, Dora wrote poetry as well. In 1911, she created *Farmikins Farm Rhymes*, a book of verse that was also set to music. Dora dedicated the book of children's poems to her son.

"Dedicated to my small boy, Verne. Through whose eyes I am again seeing the wonders of childhood on the farm." A glimpse of Mrs. Stockman's view of her small son is seen in this poem.

---

[118] Westley 82

Farmerkin

Farmerkin, Farmerkin,
Happy little boy,
With your Wonder-World
Brimming full of joy.

Running through the dewy fields,
Playing in the brook,
Finding nuts and berries,
Knows each mossy nook.
Friends of all the animals
Learning how they grow,
Digging, planting, sowing,
Watching flowers blow.

Farmerkin, Farmerkin,
In wonder-World of joy
Who would not wish to be,
A little farmer boy? [119]

State Grange Lecturer

In 1913, Stockman was selected by Michigan Governor Woodbridge N. Ferris to serve as a delegate to international Congress of Farm Women. The group met in November, in Tulsa, Oklahoma. This was strong recognition by the governor of Dora's ability and exceptional communication skills. A major public-speaking opportunity was to last sixteen years. In 1914, Dora Stockman was elected as State Grange Lecturer and served

---

[119] Stockman 13, *courtesy of the Stockman family*

until 1930. This department of the State Grange carried a great deal of responsibility. Her mandate was to educate and inform. The meeting plans were to be used in every local Grange hall. She set the tone for meetings throughout the state and traveled widely throughout the state attending local Grange meetings, district meetings, Pamona Grange and statewide meeting for the Patrons of Husbandry.

Award from Governor Ferris to International Congress of Women. *Michigan State University Archives and Historical Collections*

Stockman also served as chair to the home economics committee for the organization within the State of Michigan. As a state lecturer, she was invited to speak on Grange Day on the topic of Rural Leadership. This was part of the four great conferences taking place at Bay View near Petosky, Michigan. Dora appeared as part of the country life program on Country Life Days.

A distinguishing feature of the Bay View season is a series of annual conferences on great themes of human welfare, and participated in by men and women who are leaders in their special department. First in order, always, comes the Bible Conference, which is a practical adaptation of the old Camp Meeting to changed condition.[120]

In addition to the conferences, educational programs included a wide range of topics. Bay View Summer University

---

[120] Bay View Assembly

Bay View Bulletin. *Courtesy of the Stockman family.*

included several areas of study during the six-week program. Continuing education for teachers in language arts, music, and physical education classes were popular with instructors hired from Oberlin College. More specifically, the opportunities for teachers included an emphasis on Kindergarten Methods for Teachers. The program provided a laboratory opportunity through a supervised kindergarten for children. Methods courses at the primary and grammar level were also available. A course in storytelling methods and in playground and recreation work was also included. A wide array of courses included arts and crafts. Under the heading of "Woman's Work," cooking and domestic arts together with a course in millinery were also offered.

This well-known Michigan resort area continues to draw visitors today as it did in 1915. However, in 1915, the modes of transportation were more often by steamship or railroad than by the current use of automobiles, vans, and buses.

Public Speaking

Significant advancements in science, industry, and organization followed the period of Reconstruction leading into the Progressive Era in America. Before this era, there existed the isolated communities: "America during the nineteenth century was a society of island communities. Weak communication

56

severely restricted the interaction among these islands" and healthy survival depended upon "its ability to manage the lives of its members" and the "belief among its members that the community had such powers."[121] The work provides a structural framework to understand the economic demands of a nation that would eventually support the growing educational needs of Americans.

In the last quarter of the nineteenth century, there was a need for articulate public speakers. "Interest in popular education was tied to two factors associated with that period—industrialization and nationalism."[122] Effective platform speakers had typically been the leaders in the community and often included ministers and politicians. Nevertheless, there was simply not a large enough pool of people who could speak and persuade effectively. Manufacturers, for example, needed a sales force that could sell the types of merchandise being readied by industry for the mass market. Furthermore, there was a need for articulate and persuasive speakers who could provide leadership in the workplace and in the community associations that were a growing part of democracy, as Alexis deTocqueville had observed in his travels:

> Americans enjoyed their associations with one another. Amongst democratic nations all the citizens are independent and feeble; they can hardly do anything by themselves, and none of them oblige his fellowmen to lend him their assistance. They all, therefore, become powerless, if they do not learn voluntarily to help each other.[123]

---

[121] WIEBE XIII

[122] STOCK 126

[123] deTocqueville 199

The burgeoning labor unions required speakers who could unite a group for action. Associations were forming for mutual protection in many spheres, including education. In a democracy, this generally requires consensus building. It was no longer the island community but corporate industry and civil government that needed to marshal people behind their causes. Effective speakers were needed to equip and train students for roles and behaviors heretofore unimagined. Thus, the bridge between economic necessity and education was created through the employment of effective public-speaking.

Before the Civil War, high schools were confined to cities. In 1857, they existed in eighty cities. There was little uniformity of curriculum even within individual states. The best offered English, humanities, algebra, geometry, natural sciences, Latin and sometimes, Greek. Programs ranged anywhere from one to four years.[124]

The inclusion of the rural students after the Civil War represented a marked change. "The earliest reliable statistics, in 1890, show that there were 202,963 pupils in public high schools."[125] According to one Grange chronicler, "Preferring town to farm life, the Stockmans 'put a man on the farm' and moved to Lansing in 1914 when she began her long service as Lecturer of the State Grange."[126] Putting a man on the farm appeared to have given Stockman more free time for Grange activities. "The 42nd annual session at Battle Creek in December 1914 was noteworthy in at least one important respect. That

---

[124] Stock 187
[125] Stock 188

[126] Marti, *Women of the Grange: Mutuality and Sisterhood in Rural America 127*

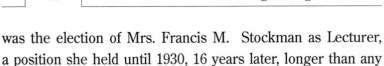
was the election of Mrs. Francis M. Stockman as Lecturer, a position she held until 1930, 16 years later, longer than any other Michigan state Grange Lecturer."[127]

Free public libraries, paperbound books and periodicals were available in abundance. The progress of the traveling libraries in a national Grange publication was described: "At present there are some 500 of these traveling libraries in use in Granges, Farmers' Clubs, Women's Clubs, etc. The State Librarian will also assist Granges who wish to purchase books in making wise selections and in securing discounts."[128]

However, the Grangers were frustrated with the limitations imposed on rural education. "Grange comparisons had made them aware that school terms and teachers' salaries in the farming regions were seldom comparable to those in the urban centers. Furthermore, their children usually did not have the same high school opportunities."[129]

Education was often promoted through the lecture method and pithy phrases or slogans. As an outgrowth of increased emphasis upon education, newspapers became an increasingly popular source of information for the rural family. "Due to the increase in circulation, newspaper and magazine publishers frequently cooperated with the Grange by offering special club rates to all members of the organization."[130]

Suspicion decreased for those who had previously been outsiders in the Grange Hall. A new respect was forged for the college professor, who was a welcome lecturer on farm topics. "In addition to its own activities, the Grange in cooperation with the state agricultural colleges and with the experiment stations

---

[127] Trump 101

[128] Holden 51

[129] Nordin, *Mainstreams of Grangerism: A Revisionist View of the Order of Patrons of Husbandry 74*

[130] Nordin, *Mainstreams of Grangerism: A Revisionist View of the Order of Patrons of Husbandry 21–22*

also established farmer institutes."[131]

Scientific wonders of the age seen at the Columbian Exposition excited an audience with its exhibits. Public-speaking did not escape the influence of science. The Del Sartre Method sought to codify the gestures of emotions so that they might be studied and replicated by students and turn out effective speakers with coordination and grace. Coordination and grace would be useful skills in an ever-shrinking world of the future.

In the 1890s, there was a rationale for public-speaking and the art of persuasion. Training was required to compose and deliver an address. Eventually public-speaking in some guise became a graduation expectation. Whether it was called elocution/speech, or rhetoric/persuasion, it was nonetheless an important ingredient for progress for both urban and rural citizens.

Increased urbanization moved people closer and closer together. The middle-class was growing. Labor was migrating at a swift pace from Europe as the first wave of skilled workers arrived and quickly filled the void. "Where the industrial revolution had taken place, education was regarded as necessary to prepare people to operate in a highly complex society, and give them the skills and discipline required by mechanization."[132]

The second wave of refugees was somewhat less skilled and flooded the cities, overburdening the social, economic, and educational systems. The skilled workers and long-standing citizens moved further from the center of the city, and workers migrated from the farm. "As a by-product, it was hoped that schooling would ameliorate the social problems brought on by urbanization—vice, crime, abandonment of children,

---

[131] Nordin, *Rich Harvest: A History of the Grange* 26   [132] Stock 126

prostitution."[133] The motives for education at the turn of the century echoed the aims of education from colonial times in its linkage to morality. "In the English colonies in America, education was regarded highly, as a means of insuring religious orthodoxy and of integrating youth into a new society."[134] The struggle continued.

Cultural Assimilation

While Stockman was at work in the rural community, urban settings had their organizers too. The influence of Jane Addams as an urban reformer at Hull House in Chicago was notable. She encouraged young people to participate and join social clubs. Addams also used the arts to forestall the despair of the urban life. In her book, *Twenty Years at Hull House*, Addams described the usefulness of the social clubs: "On the whole we were much impressed by the great desire for self-improvement, for study and debate, exhibited by many of the young men." Addams noted with a touch of sadness the near over-achievement reached by the members of the former members of the social clubs: "Of course there were many disappointments connected with these clubs when the rewards of political and commercial life easily drew the members away from the principles advocated in club meetings."[135]

The arts at Hull House included commercial art, painting, music, and theater. Addams chronicled the effects of squandering musical talents by overwork in factories and overexposure in the Vaudeville houses, along with the ignorance of parents.[136] Melodrama was quite attractive to the members of Hull House.

---

[133] Stock 126

[134] Stock 73

[135] Addams 239

[136] Addams 241

Addams describes the allure of the art form: "The universal desire for the portrayal of life lying quite outside of personal experience evinces itself in many forms. One of the conspicuous features of our neighborhood, as of all industrial quarters, is the persistency with which the entire population attends the theater."[137] Addams continued:

> The sort of melodrama they see there has recently been described as "The ten commandments written in red fire." Certainly the villain always comes to a violent end, and the young and handsome hero is rewarded by marriage with a beautiful girl, usually the daughter of a millionaire, but after all that is not a portrayal of the morality of the Ten Commandments any more than of life itself.[138]

Addams described the enthusiasm experienced by the participants in the drama program: "The young people's clubs never tired of rehearsing and preparing for these dramatic occasions, and we also discovered that older people were almost equally ready and talented."[139] Challenges to cultural assimilation are noted in these comments by Addams about a play that illustrates this point. "I recall a play, written by an Italian playwright of our neighborhood, which depicted the insolent break between Americanized sons and old country parents so touchingly that it moved to tears all the older Italians in the audience."[140]

In the city, women, exempt as they were from masculine aggressiveness, could band together to create a better world.

---

[137] Addams 264–265

[138] Addams 266

[139] Addams 267

[140] Addams 269

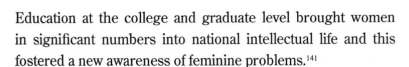

Education at the college and graduate level brought women in significant numbers into national intellectual life and this fostered a new awareness of feminine problems.[141]

Study clubs for women became a popular resource of acceptable settings for women to participate in educational and social activities. "Beginning immediately after the Civil War and continuing for the next twenty to thirty years, women, at an amazing rate and often unaware that their 'sisters' were doing likewise, formed study clubs almost identical in structure, purpose, and operation."[142] The activities of the clubs anticipated the idea of lifelong learning. Women used the outlet available to them for affiliation and contemplation through education in the study club. "Although the women who joined study clubs were seldom 'aimless, ignorant, and hopeless,' they were women for whom the colleges of that time could in fact do nothing."[143]

A woman in this era was also encouraged to become more involved with the scientific management of the home. However, there could be sharp contrasts between the type of domestic life a woman might experience if her husband decided to homestead rather than remain in an urban setting.

Theatrical Enterprise

Theatrical enterprise during the Progressive Era in American history harbored the spirit of vitality and possibility for the professional and amateur alike. Whether in city, town, village, or rural community, the entertainment brought a rich opportunity for education and enjoyment. The time from approximately 1865 to 1925 included a variety of possibilities

---

[141] Addams

[142] Martin 14

[143] Martin 83

for both performer and audience member.

Before describing the plays of Stockman written for the Grange, it is necessary to understand the background of the American theater experience. Theatrical conditions were noted by de Tocqueville during his travels in America. The theatrical movements of melodrama and realism are explored for their influence upon the plays of the Grange written by Stockman. The theatrical enterprise of Vaudeville is included for its influences on the development of taste by the audience. Dramatic literature of the period will include the explanation of the well-made-play and audience reception to this type of presentation during the Progressive Era. The final portion considers the training available for performers of the era.

Western theater in America at the turn of the century enjoyed a plethora of options. The classic plays of Greece and Rome together with the European and British imports stood alongside the remarkable domestic fare then available. From melodrama to Vaudeville, the American audience could encounter a variety of emotional experiences in the towns and cities. The lights of Broadway echoed throughout the country in imitation of the grand theatrical houses. Other performance space stretched the imagination of a more remote audience who watched events in town halls, Grange Halls, tents, saloons, and barns. The minimum requirements for a performance included a play, a playing space, and an audience.

Alexis de Tocqueville traveled extensively in America in 1831, including a wilderness trek through Michigan. His remarks, based upon observations of people and events in America, have provided a wealth of insights into the North American experience. More specifically, his comments on theater in America provide a useful framework for appreciation

of amateur theater.

Documented amateur theatrical activity has been noted since the performance in 1665 of *Ye Bear and Ye Cub*.[144] Amateur theater has been a part of local community efforts, civic organizations, private clubs, and even some churches. Nevertheless, within the general confines of the period from 1865 to 1925, the discussion will be narrowed to the work of a unique American institution and its use of amateur theater.

A prophetic year, 1865, found Americans living through historical milestones such as the assassination of Lincoln and the ending of the U. S. Civil War. Theatrically, David Belasco, at the age of 12, was performing in *Jim Black*, or *The Regulator's Revenge*. Daily life was eased with the invention of the ice-making machine around 1854 and the carpet sweeper. Long distance travel also eased with the creation of the Pullman sleeping car, and Maria Mitchell was appointed as professor of astronomy at Vassar College. It was a new beginning for America. A progressive age was to continue with limited economic setbacks until the First World War. It was an age of world travel for those who could afford such luxuries. A traveler in 1888 with a box camera could travel the world and see firsthand the wonders of past ages. The wonders of the past could be captured on film and shared with others.

While deTocqueville's tour of America was ostensibly to study the American prison system, his work, *Democracy In America*, became a comprehensive examination of American social, cultural, and political institutions. His comments on the theater are useful in understanding the plays written for the Grange:

---

[144] Vardac 281

Authors will aim at rapidity of execution, more than at perfection of detail. Small productions will be more common than bulky books: there will be more wit than erudition, more imagination than profundity; and literary performances will bear marks of an untutored and rude vigor of thought, frequently of great variety and singular fecundity.[145]

Other comments by the French writer include his observations that theater's purpose is to "provide literary gratification to the multitudes" and that "little or no study is required to enjoy American theatre."[146] He noticed, too, that social classes mixed in the theater and that it was an immediate theater, that is, American theater presented not the plays of ancient subjects but what was of present concern or interest to an American audience.

Other thoughts on the theater included deTocqueville's views on the lack of a common rule for theater due to distance between people and places. He also observed that American theater is noted for its "keen emotions of the heart and not the pleasures of the mind."[147] This view suggests a ready reception for the melodrama that was to become a popular genre. Perhaps that is what accounts for yet another observation of deTocqueville's, the habit of bridging problems through matrimony.

An additional note on the theater of the fledgling America is that plays were intended to be performed rather than read. Capturing the imagination of the audience was a novelty in performance known as realism. Realism in America seemed

---

[145] deTocqueville 177
[146] Bently 479

[147] Bently 483

most appropriate for a burgeoning nation. Realism was evident not only in photography and staging but in paintings and sculpture as well. While it may not have been possible for everyone to travel, it was possible, with technology, to mass-produce quite cheaply the sculpture "Wounded Scout." In 1864, this union soldier no doubt contributed to the rising sense of nationalism after the Civil War. The sculpture was realistic. Photographs produced in magazines and newspapers provided windows to the world.

The first recorded American female playwright was Anna Cora Mowatt. Mowatt's play, *Fashion,* reflected the current upper-class social behaviors of the day; it also mirrored the political and social climate of the mid-1800s in America. During the antebellum period, prosperity was on the rise for the ambitious. The city, aside from all its detractions, could foster a positive arena for change in the way women viewed themselves.[148]

Innovative creative artists in realistic American staging included Steele MacKaye and David Belasco. Kenneth MacGowan attributes the playwriting pioneering of realism in America to Steele MacKaye. The 1880 play, *Hazel Kirke,* is described as a "domestic drama with a quiet naturalness."[149] While the previous acting style had been bombastic and largely imported from abroad, the new scripting required a different approach to acting, a more natural, realistic style. "The picture-frame stage has come with the intimate drama, with the play which appeals through slight gesture and pregnant sentences that make their insistent demand upon the quick appreciation of the audiences."[150]

---

[148] Conway

[149] MacGowan, *Footlights Across America* 393

[150] Quinn 49

Steele MacKaye was quite taken with the work of Francois Delsarte, who was advocating a naturalistic style of performance in the theater with reproducible codified gestures. MacKaye's contributions to the realism upon the stage were not limited, however, to improvements in scripts and acting style alone. MacKaye was responsible for innovations in stage design and equipment that increased the speed at which scenes could be changed. The result of these improvements contributed to the new pictorial imagery.[151]

Realism

Realism upon the stage could dazzle an audience with the seemingly very ordinary becoming extraordinary. Critically-acclaimed theatrical director and designer Belasco is quoted as saying the "incidents are selected from among the unusual episodes of an ordinary life."[152] Lighting, a natural part of life, was to play a major part in Belasco's creative work, and he was given credit for doing away with the footlights entirely and the use of dimmers along with the use of individual lamps on the balcony rail that ultimately led to effects that are more realistic. For example, the audience must have been captivated in *Girl of the Golden West*, when blood dripped from the loft above the girl's cabin loft as the sheriff searched for the escaping bandit lying wounded in the loft. The excitement was immediate. There was no delayed gratification. Not only was Belasco attempting to capture realism in language, characters and the set, but he was also providing a view of a segment of the country that not everyone would know firsthand. The realism on the stage could transport an audience member from the city

---

[151] MacGowan, *Footlights Across America* 397   [152] Quinn 197

to the country, providing immediate glimpses into another part of their nation.

David Belasco was a master of realistic staging. Commenting on the frustrations of the theatrical enterprise, Belasco held forth on a number of areas including his comments on women playwrights: "It is a common impulse of sentimental women to want to write plays, and thousands of them try."[153] He declared, "The first law of the stage is to convince the audience of the truth and logic of the work."[154] Truth and logic did not exclude emotion, however, as in this comment: "The secret is that it is much easier to appeal to the hearts of audiences through their senses than through their intellects."[155]

The stage is a mirror in which are reflected the manners and peculiarities of life of its contemporaneous day. So drama is always affected to a large degree by the thought and by the social, political and economic customs of the generation from which it springs.[156]

The new pictorial imagery presented on the stage by the spectacular realism of Belasco and others was presenting the audience with reflections of their own life experiences or more exciting events, which could be experienced vicariously.

Contemporaries of Belasco, besides Steele MacKaye, included Herbert Beer-Bohm as well as George M. Cohan who "wrote musical comedies that were fast, wholesome and filled with a sweet odor of sentimental patriotism. The idol of middle-class playgoers."[157]

---

[153] Belasco 42
[154] Belasco 50
[155] Belasco 74–75

[156] Belasco 229
[157] Lynes 146

It is that same spirit of realistic enterprise that Stockman included in her plays for the Patrons of Husbandry. The types of plays that were abroad in the land were reflected in the scripts for the Juvenile Grange. Her zeal for representing life's truth is discovered in the writings and reflections of the Bard of the Grange.

5

The Grange Bard
1917-1918

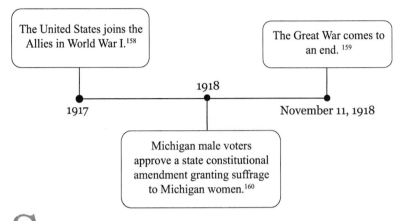

The United States joins the Allies in World War I.[158]

The Great War comes to an end. [159]

1918

1917

November 11, 1918

Michigan male voters approve a state constitutional amendment granting suffrage to Michigan women.[160]

Stockman brought a unique perspective to the world of theatrical enterprise. She discovered a need for change in her pioneering work for the Grange and established herself as a change agent by participating within the sphere available to a woman of her time. This was not the theater audience described in *Town Hall* with three stories of entrepreneurial enterprise situated in small towns throughout America. Moreover, while farmers may have had occasion to visit the merchants on the first floor or the offices on the second floor, they were generally far too remote to travel to meeting halls for cultural activities with their families.

Sensitive to the needs of her audience, she created an opportunity for distilling knowledge with drama. Her work in the field of drama represents yet another outlet for her creative

---

[158] *Chronology of Michigan Women's History*   [160] *Chronology of Michigan Women's History*
[159] *This Date in Michigan History*

71

energies. The Stockman plays contain elements common in social problem plays, melodramas, and the well-made plays.

Grange Playwright

It was not all work and no play for the farm families. The types of entertainment available to agrarian communities display a picture of some of the long-established theatrical conventions. The rural family had to create their own entertainment in their own settings. What better place to perform than at the Grange Hall! If the construction guidelines for the hall had been financially and faithfully followed, a stage might already be in place. Theatrical production had to be homegrown too. Grange playwright Stockman followed in the footsteps of the American pioneer tradition in creating an amateur production. Stereotyping of rural life has been a popular sport since earliest recorded time. The poor country bumpkin in American playwriting became a theatrical cliché, as did the Yankee character. There is a need to exercise care when judging the work of the rural writer Stockman.

The motives for creating plays for a rural audience stemmed from the goals for the Patrons of Husbandry. Stockman's goal in using plays was to provide a way of conveying an educational ideal in an entertaining manner. It was a vehicle to educate and communicate the message of the Patrons of Husbandry, and it further provided training in public-speaking through performance. Stockman's plays included popular theatrical conventions such as melodrama, and many of the elements of the well-made play. Finally, the plays of Stockman represented real social problems faced by the Patron's of Husbandry.

Melodrama

A popular theatrical staple is the use of the melodrama, and an excellent example is the temperance theme in *Ten Nights in a Bar-room*. "The battles of melodrama are all external, thus making this dramatic genre highly dependent on forces beyond the control of the protagonist."[161] The world of the melodramatic play is unequivocal. "It is the world as we would like it to be, with clear choices, definite villains, and always a happy ending for the deserving."[162] In spite of theatrical criticism, melodramatic productions were popular and Stockman's melodramas were no exception.

Stockman's longest play, *The Coming of Happy Valley Grange to Hard Scrabble Hollow,* is an opportunity to discuss the merits of joining the Grange through melodrama. The play illustrates the effects of the Grange on a forlorn farm family. This is the longest extant play that Stockman wrote for the Grange. The play opened in Grange Rapids before members of the National Grange in 1919, according to Jeannie Buell, author of *The Grange Master and Grange Lecturer.* She described the play in this way: "It has been the means in many other states of leading scores of outsiders to see the Grange as an educational institution in a true and broad sense, and as such interpretation of the Order, this little play ranks among the finest flower of Grange literature."[163] The script itself is undated but its cover indicates that it was written for the State Grange by the State Lecturer, Mrs. Dora H. Stockman, and given by members of the Charlotte Grange, at the State Grange session held in Lansing. Clearly, Stockman anticipated a wide audience for the script,

---

[161] Grose and Kenworthy

[162] Grose and Kenworthy 369

[163] Buell 114

at least among the Grange. "This can easily be adapted to any Grange and will be sold for 10 cents a copy to Grange people outside the Michigan Grange."[164] A brief overview of the story clearly conveys the didactic nature of the melodrama.

Dora described her characters as Mrs. Frost, an overworked farm woman; Mr. Frost, badly in debt with poor show for crops; daughter Florence, who aspires to sing; and Mr. Goodhue, Grange Deputy, bringing helpful information to the Frost family about farming. In addition to these four characters, two other roles complete the cast in the full-length script: Son, Johnny Frost, a young boy who makes things interesting; and last, but by no means least, Guy Wood, a prosperous young farmer from Hillcrest and a neighbor who is interested in Florence Frost.

The setting for this play is the Frost family kitchen. The Frosts are troubled, complaining and arguing with their children. Johnny begs to visit the Grange meeting, and the parents will not give permission, indicating that it is a waste of time. Meanwhile, her parents have likewise turned down daughter Florence, who also wants to attend a Grange meeting, where she has been invited to sing. In her despair, she is lured to talk to a stranger from Chicago who offers her a chance to sing in the chorus in Chicago. She indicates that she does not have the carfare, whereupon he produces a train ticket from Grand Rapids to Chicago. He convinces her that she should just slip away and not tell the folks. She is in such despair over her dismal farm life that she accepts. Meanwhile Mr. Goodhue, the Grange Deputy, is visiting the family of the Frosts, discussing and describes the merits of Grange membership.[165]

The next act of *Happy Valley* notes the passing of three

---

[164] D. Stockman, *The Coming of Happy Valley Grange to Hard Scrabble Hollow*

[165] D. Stockman, *The Coming of Happy Valley Grange to Hard Scrabble Hollow*

years and the transformed household through the offices of participation in the Grange. Guy Wood proposes to Florence Frost after learning that she would not be heading off to the Metropolitan Theater on Broadway if her parents had not invested so much money on her voice training. She reveals that she loves rural life more than the career that lies ahead for her. The play concludes with a plan for the Grange Hall wedding.

The play took the lives of common people seriously and paid much respect to their superior purity and wisdom. It elevated them often into aristocracy, always into a world charged with action, excitement, and a sense of wonder. It gave audiences a chance to empathize in a direct way, to laugh and to cry, and it held up ideals and promised rewards, particularly that of the paradise of the happy home based on female purity, that were available to all.[166]

Well-Made Play

The Stockman plays are rural melodramas in the vein of a well-made-play, a popular form of playwriting eschewed by the critics but drawing wide acceptance with a popular audience. This type of play was popularly embraced but artistically despised. The seemingly magical formula of Eugene Scribe's well-made play provided a road map for generations of playwrights to follow. While the journey for subsequent writers was somewhat checkered, the final destination has yet to be determined as the legacy of the well-made play continues.

The formula worked out by the early nineteenth-century writer was embraced by other popular playwrights and continued to be reflected in popular media of the twentieth

---

[166] Grimsted 248

century. Certainly, the circumstances were artificial, and there was intrigue built around some striking situations.

While the criticism of the well-made play was rampant and characterized it as being slick and melodramatic, many of the critics made use of the formula's better elements. Scribe was attempting to hold the attention of the audience completely from beginning to the end of the play.[167]

Among the several elements of the well-made play, there was an inclusion and demonstration of popular technology of the day. In addition to contemporary technology, contemporary events were also a convention of the well-made play. Among the features of a well-made play is a plot based on a secret known to the audience, but not to the major characters—the secret will be revealed to them in the climatic scene. Still another feature of the well-made play is a plot that is the culmination of a long story, most of which has happened before the curtain has gone up.

The building of suspense is yet another hallmark of the well-made play. Using contrived entrances, exits, letters, and revelations of identities, the audience remains attentive. Yet another convention of Scribe's well-made-play is the hero or protagonist who is in conflict with an adversary who experiences alternately good and bad turns of fortune, thereby giving rhythm to the play. Finally, the well-made play contains some definite plot prescriptions: exposition in the first act, a situation in the second, and the unraveling in the third. The usefulness of the well-made play is clear. Playwrights can reflect unique themes and problems of their time, providing an audience with informative entertainment in a well-made way. The formula continues in the popular theater of the early twenty-first century

---

[167] Grose and Kenworthy 371

carried out in contemporary media.

Social Problem Plays

The history of dramatic literature is filled with examples of social problem plays. Among the many period pieces are several titles illustrating this point: *Luke the Laborer,* 1826; *The Silver King,* 1882; *The Corsican Brothers,* 1852; *Let's Get A Divorce,* 1880; *A Woman of No Importance,* 1893; and *Girl of the Golden West,* 1905.

Stockman's plays are not unusual in light of the foregoing. What is unique is the particular purpose, audience, and setting for her work. What she shares in common with the popular plays are the women as catalysts for action. These plays also provided many opportunities for dramatic action by women. The dialogue of the plays gives credence to Dora's recognition of the problem of migration to the cities. She further clarified the problems of the youth on farms in the dialogues of the *Happy Valley* play. Stockman was acting as a change agent influencing the lives of those who read, performed, and viewed her plays. The legacy of plays within the Grange movement was a recognized attempt to entertain and to educate.

The Coming of Happy Valley Grange to Hard Scrabble Hollow was probably a real crowd-pleaser for Grange members because it extolled the virtues and values of rural life, and, more importantly, endorsed continued support for Grange Hall activities. The Grange, as demonstrated in *Happy Valley,* provided an outlet for the many dreams of young people in America. Granted, the enlightenment of the audience was rather transparent in these plays. There is, for example, the reinforcement of the idea that strangers should be feared and avoided and that the city's ability to lure youth away from the farm resulted in grave economic consequences to the remaining farm families. It was her goal to provide a wholesome environment in Happy Valley and elsewhere. Before the movies eclipsed the popular theater of the day, plays remained for families. Subtle shifts in what was acceptable or interesting for an audience occurred.

Options to participate in dramatic performance at any level encouraged still further interest in dramatic training and elocution. While people might not be stars and obtain top billing, nonetheless, participation in the theatrical enterprise was quite engaging and was excellent training for public speaking. In the last quarter of the nineteenth century, there was an abundant need for articulate spokesmen.

Education and training in public speaking and in the performing arts was also an ongoing activity. Contrary to popular belief, theatrical instruction was available in America before Constantine Stanislavsky. "We have been brainwashed into thinking that significant actor training in America did not exist prior to the arrival of Stanislavsky in 1923. During the period between 1875 and 1925, America was a hotbed of activity concerned with the elusive principles that underlie acting."[168] The apprentice method, which had been the standard theatrical training since its earliest days in ancient Greece, was replaced by several evolutions in design. The stock companies provided a method of formal apprenticeship.

In saluting the valuable contributions to the Grange by Michigan women, Dora H. Stockman is referenced as a state lecturer and writer on home and agricultural topics. Stockman

---

[168] McTeague, *Before Stanislavsky: American Professional Acting Schools and Acting Theory*

"instituted among the Grange children of the state a number of 'Four Leaf Clover Clubs,' which served a useful purpose in the way of entertainment, character development and education of the children."[169] The 4-H Clubs throughout the country today are a legacy of Stockman's creation.

Stockman's dissertation draft profiles the relationship of children in the life of the local Grange Hall meeting. In a section labeled "Young People and Children in the Grange," Stockman reflects on the integral nature of children and the Grange.

From its earliest history, it has been an attractive rural community center for the entire family. It has been quite customary for Granges to provide a place for the children at Grange meetings. As a very young child, the author can remember standing up on the bed that was built in the alcove of the Grange Hall to provide for the children, and joining in the singing in the opening of the Grange. A Children's Day program has been in vogue since early in the 80's; State Master Lute, later Governor of Michigan, designated a day in June as Children's Day. Most Granges observe this day on their programs when the children of Grange families and usually children of the school and community take part on the Lecturer's program.[170] Other titles of Stockman's plays represent an interesting profile of the focus of attention for the Grange audience:

A Modern Hero

A Patriotic Party
An Old Fashioned Mother
Blossom's Letter to Santa Claus

---

[169] Gardner, *The Grange—Friend of the Farmer 216*

[170] D. Stockman, *Women in the Grange*

Brownies and Fairies on a Strike
Dr. Mary's Prescription
Hero Worshipers
Neenah's Gratitude
Santa Claus Visits the Williams Family
Santa Clause Junior Substitute
The Golden Wedding
The Hope of Israel
The Report of the Thanksgiving Dinner
The Old and the New Santa Claus.

These plays were useful educational tools for instructing children as well as adults. An example illustrates the point. *Dr. Mary's Prescription* is set in a farm home; the characters focus attention on health care practices. The farm family women are discouraged from using unorthodox methods of health care.

The play opens with Grandmother suggesting herbal teas for a fussy baby. A patent medicine is suggested by one of the women. Another believes that Baled Marsh Hay is the answer. The problem is solved with the arrival of a cousin who is doing post-doctoral studies at a university. After examining the contents of the patent medicine, she decries their uses and points to science and education to improve life. A subplot is the diagnosis of Matilda's drug dependency after analysis of Matilda's medicine. Recognizing her problem, Matilda vows to never touch another drop of medicine without a doctor's prescription. This is a didactic play, conveying useful information for the audience.

The end neatly solves the problems raised at the beginning. The entrance of each character provides an opportunity for exposition of a problem. The major theme of the play suggested that one should not be taken in by old remedies; but instead, look to science and education to improve life.

The play contains character names that reflect the occupation or personality or interest of the person. Aunt Diet, who tries all new foods, and Doctor Bugham, a patent-medicine peddler, are two examples of this old theatrical device. The method quickly telegraphs to the audience the characters' particular perspectives.

The play is simply drawn, without a great deal of filler. It is suggestive of rural values, rituals of women in the home, and their obligations for the care and nurturing of children. The theme of the evils of drugs is reinforced several times throughout the play. The plays also reflect the progressive era in which they were crafted. For instance, *Dr. Mary's Prescription*, a play about a female doctor continuing in advanced degree work at a university, may be viewed as an endorsement for women in higher education. In addition, the theme of drug dependency among rural young women is an acknowledgment of the existing problem.

Stockman further clarified the problems of the youth on farms in the dialogues of the *Happy Valley* play. She acted as a change agent influencing the lives of those who read, performed, and viewed her plays. The legacy of plays within the Grange movement was a recognized vehicle to entertain and to educate. It was her goal to provide a wholesome environment in Happy Valley and elsewhere.

Perhaps the emergence of the Grange stage was the counterpart of what has become the new information highway of today, introducing the concept of education in a wholesome environment—the home in which the tools are the computer, much as farm implements plowed into the future. The home, in many cases, has once again become the center of education as families participate in home-schooling. Boundaries expand exponentially through the use of the online realm, creating opportunities for all citizens.

Paradoxically, the very progressive ideas represented in Stockman's writing were eventually to lead to the increase in production, and with increased production there was a diminution of the need for the family farm. Though Stockman waved the banner and encouraged youth to remain on the farm, the very success of North American farming led to the mass exodus, in spite of her very best efforts.

6

Michigan State College
1919-1931

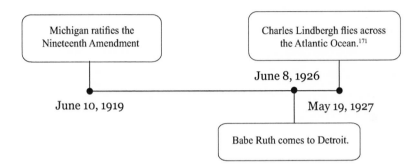

Michigan ratifies the Nineteenth Amendment

Charles Lindbergh flies across the Atlantic Ocean.[171]

June 8, 1926

June 10, 1919

May 19, 1927

Babe Ruth comes to Detroit.

Dora Stockman was at the forefront of women's suffrage in Michigan. Her election to public office in Michigan made the record books in 1919. She later managed to turn defeat in a state-wide Grange election into a successful run for the State House. In between these two victories, her work continued for the progressive aims of agriculture. Throughout her time in office on the State Board of Agriculture, she broadened her appeal to an even wider audience through continued public speaking, radio broadcasting, and musical composing. This very productive period included work for the *Michigan Patron* and the beginning of a doctoral degree in sociology.

Woman's Suffrage

While the role of women on the farm was often bleak, an effort was made to confront some of the hardships of that life

---

[171] *This Date in Michigan History*

through woman's suffrage. "Woman's Suffrage had made its first advances where it was seen as a protection of home and community, particularly in the Yankee version."[172] Through membership in the Grange and evangelizing for the Women's Christian Temperance Union (WCTU), Dora was an ideal candidate to seek a larger forum for her ideas. As a proficient public speaker, she could address a variety of issues important to the family. "The club movement and the increasing prominence of women in causes such as temperance and control of prostitution marked the emergence of the middle-class American woman into a position of ongoing influence in American public life."[173]

In November of 1918, a state amendment granted women suffrage two years before the Federal 19th Amendment. [174] On April 7, 1919, Dora Stockman was the first woman elected to state-wide public office in Michigan. She was elected to serve on the State Board of Agriculture for a six-year term, "at a time when woman's suffrage was new and no one gave a woman candidate much of a chance. But every farmer and farmer's wife in Michigan knew her personally or knew of her efforts on their behalf. She was elected April 7, 1919, by a plurality of 288,447, for a six-year term." [175] Ultimately, she served on the State Board of Agriculture for two terms—a total of twelve years. The shift or structural transformation of American values from small town 1880's to a new bureaucratic-minded middle-class by 1920 represented a dramatic change. It moved America away from many people making small decisions to a few people talking about big issues. Dora Stockman entered into the swift current of public office in Michigan before the federal amendment granted women the right to vote, let alone

---

[172] D. Morgan 17
[173] D. Morgan 20

[174] O'Rourke-Kelly 88
[175] Darling 22

seek public office.

Dora was by now a long way from the log home of her birth. She was now to realize a campaign goal while serving on the Board of Agriculture. In the next phase of her life's work, with her usual zeal for mission on behalf of the family, Dora advanced the cause of women in a material way. She had a clear mandate from the sisters of the Grange. Relationship with the Grange continued throughout this period. The strength of her constituency was drawn from the countless numbers of women whom she had met in her Grange work as State Lecturer and through her writings for *The Michigan Patron*. The women were solidly behind their "Sister Dora." There were many items of mutual concern to the Sisters of the Grange. Education and equal participation were central themes.

Board of Agriculture

Dora Stockman was elected to the Board of Agriculture in 1919 and again in 1925, which then controlled the Michigan Agricultural College now known as Michigan State University. This was no small feat. *The Detroit Free Press* feature section headline read, "Michigan Women Backward in Taking Office Hold fewer than 350 political positions out of 11,500 of varying importance, according to records of League of Women Voters."[176] The article also noted Dora Stockman's unusual achievement: "Although women repeatedly have been candidates in state-wide elections for state office, only one has achieved victory— Mrs. Dora Stockman, of Lansing, member of the state board of agriculture, involving as it does a voice in the administration of Michigan State College. Mrs. Stockman's victories have been

---

[176] "Michigan Women Backward in Taking Office"

impressive."[177]

The need for a trained labor market was quickly becoming evident as colleges, graduate, and professional schools came into being. While there had been colleges, seminaries, and medical schools before, these were generally not available to a large segment of society before the Civil War. However, after the Civil War, educational philanthropy endowed new and old institutions; increased funding made research and graduate study possible.

The Morrill Act of 1862 created land-grant colleges "for liberal and practical education of the industrial classes in the several pursuits and professions of life."[178] The land-grant colleges were generally available to a limited number of students who had the time and money to afford the taking of a degree. Initially, the Grangers' view on higher education was that "the members could not tolerate anything but agriculture being taught at these institutions, and they were suspicious of the 'classical departments.' "[179] The friends of agriculture were determined to gain funding for the needs of college students who were entering to study scientifically-based programs. "The Grange will not withdraw from this fight and will wage it until we have Federal aid of teaching agriculture and home economics in all the grade schools and high schools in the country, as well as good courses in the state agricultural colleges and normal schools to prepare teachers for this work."[180]

It is striking that the issues raised because of the transformational shift are problems still wrestled with today. Small-level political groups, while trying to maintain their island

---

[177] "Michigan Women Backward in Taking Office"

[178] Blauch 632

[179] Nordin, *Mainstreams of Grangerism: A Revisionist View of the Order of Patrons of Husbandry*

[180] Patterson 207

community, are impacted by the larger controlling agencies or legislative bodies. Local political groups continue to appeal to the grass roots voters in small communities.

In 1925, Dora Stockman was re-elected to the State Board of Agriculture. With Dora's six more years in office, Francis Stockman sold off registered Holstein cattle and moved into East Lansing. Another educational effort came from the distaff side. The Extension Division Reports of the 1927 State Board of Agriculture report takes note of the Women's Institute.

The Woman's Institute was the brainchild of Stockman and the report details the number of women attending and the types of activities that were available: "Two hundred rural women of Michigan attended the meeting. It was interesting to note that from ninety to ninety-five percent of the women present were either local leaders or members of local groups from counties where Home Economics projects had been in operation."[181] The women were in a leadership-training program and were participating in the short-course program while being housed in college dormitories. The program was encouraging the growth of Home Demonstration Agents. The home economics building at Michigan State University was constructed during Dora's tenure as a member of the college board of control.

While advancing the opportunities for women to approach their work in a scientific manner, she did not forget the children. She is attributed with creating the forerunner to the 4-H program through her Clover Clubs. Stockman was the "Sunshine Lady" over the radio station, WKAR, in East Lansing. For two years, she read poems and led songs for farm children.

In addition, she continued her contributions to *The Michigan Patron*. During her time of service on the State Board of

---

[181] Extension Division

Agriculture Stockman, now living in East Lansing, was serving as editor. The cover of the February, 1927, five cent edition had the following declaration:

> We declare only human life and ideals—not property interest—should be sacred in America. Therefore we oppose our government protecting property interest in foreign countries, except by arbitrates. In case of war the government should conscript property as well as men on the same basis and pay as soldiers.

The newspaper was printed monthly by the Michigan State Grange at Lansing. This notice to the reader was included with address of the Lansing, Michigan, publication office.

> While we use every effort to keep any dishonest schemer or men out of our advertising columns, we do not guarantee the reliability of our advertisers. If they don't treat you right, notify us. We will not accept "ads" for whiskey, tobacco, stock foods, patent medicine, mining stock companies, oil wells, diamonds, or any other fads or humbugs.

The lack of Michigan women in legislature was discussed in the issue. Clearly, these hints at voting for a woman presaged her own election in the next decade. The Grange lecture hour by Stockman is included. Two of Dora's poems were printed: "A Mothers Work" and "That Bothersome Boy."

Doctoral Student

In 1930, while serving on the State Board of Agriculture, at the age of 58, she began work on a doctoral degree in sociology at MSC. The title of her unfinished doctoral thesis was "The Grange and Rural Life in America." From her unfinished doctoral dissertation on the Grange, Stockman discusses a wide array of rural home concerns: heredity, home atmosphere, do and don't policy, and influence of stories and pictures. She even included a poem entitled "That Bothersome Boy" to illustrate her point. Stockman describes the merit of early literary study for children:

> Read stories to the little ones. Teach them little poems, for now is the golden opportunity for memorizing. The only Bible verses that I am absolutely sure of quoting, are the ones I learned as a little child.

> Let us have a few, but good pictures. These are the pictures that are to hang upon your child's memory walls through all his life. And, last of all, let us take time to play with our children. You cannot play with your children? You do not know how? Well, learn how. For that is the only place you can really know them and gain their confidence. No one will remember, or care, twenty years from now, whether your kitchen floor had an extra scrubbing or if Mary's dress had two ruffles or only one, but the memories of those happy days when you worked and played and really lived with your children, will then be priceless possessions. Do you think this means sacrifice to you? Yes, it does, but it is the sacrifice of Love.[182]

---

[182] D. Stockman, *The Grange and Rural Life in America*

Political Setback

While serving on the College Board of Control Stockman experienced a setback in her work for the Grange. She had attempted to become the first woman elected to the position of State Master for the Patrons of Husbandry. The close vote on the first ballot resulted in the need for a second ballot. She did not prevail but continued to build her legacy of firsts even in defeat. It was the first time in the history of the Michigan State Grange that a woman came close to being named State Master.

A newspaper account wondered what would become of Mrs. Stockman after the loss in the election for a position with the Grange leadership after twenty years of loyal service. Another newspaper account of the day reported in detail the events of the Executive Committee for the State Grange in Michigan:

> The executive committee considers Mrs. Stockman as one of the greatest workers in the order, she having organized and reorganized 31 subordinate granges in Michigan last year. The committee hopes to retain her services in some capacity. Certain developments at the

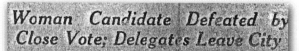

Woman Candidate Defeated by Close Vote; Delegates Leave City

George F. Roxburgh, Reed City, who for the p... headed Michigan State Grange, secured his reelectio... State...

Roxburgh Retains Post as State Master.
Source: Michigan State University Archives and Historical Collections

MRS. STOCKMAN TURNED DOWN BY STATE GRANGERS

Coldwater convention would tend to make it extremely difficult for Mrs. Stockman to work with the state master although no one questions that the East Lansing woman would do all within her power to advance the interest of the Grange since Mrs. Stockman felt quite strongly about educational issues.[183]

Surely a bitter pill to swallow with all she had done for the Grange in the past. The final paragraph described the upbeat attitude of Dora Stockman:

> Mrs. Stockman has worked day and night for the Grange for two decades and after her defeat for the mastership at Coldwater she expressed happiness over the result. She said she had "earned" a vacation. While she was humiliated by the outcome of the election she proved a good loser—a much better loser than many of her friends who were instrumental in forcing her into the mastership race.

The Bay City Daily News provided more details on the second balloting:

> The second vote was nearly as close as the first. A second ballot became necessary after the morning session Friday failed to produce the new State Master. The final count on the first vote gave neither Roxburgh nor Mrs. Stockman majorities. The second balloting took place as delegates left the convention hall during evening recess. News of Roxburgh's election came

---

[183] Runnels, *What's to Become of Mrs. Stockman?*

as a surprise to many quarters of the convention hall which delegates earlier in the day had conceded Mrs. Stockman the victory.[184]

According to a family source, that election was deeply disappointing for Dora. She had given up the role of State Lecturer in order to run for office. Rather than withdraw from public life, however, she continued down a new trail.

Revisionist writers now look back on this period of the Grange and note its limitations. Among the legacies of the Grange is the cooperative extension service that once promised to be the route of change agentry for farmers. However, even that was under question. Comments on the initial success of the program were noted: "The success of agricultural extension was based on massive public subsidies to colleges of agriculture, agricultural-experiment stations, and the related system of extension agents over more than a century."[185] The cost benefit analysis before the investment of dollars is also noted. Little consideration was given to how the effectiveness of this public investment would be measured or to what many people today would consider negative consequences of technological advances, such as the dramatic decline of jobs and small farms and the destruction of the ecological balance."[186]

State Board of Agriculture c. 1913 Michigan State College. *Source: Michigan State University Archives and Historical Collections—Dora Hall-Stockman Collection.*

Under Dora's terms of

---

[184] "Roxburgh Retains Post as State Master"

[185] Matkin

[186] Matkin

office, the home economics building was constructed. "She mobilized the farm women so well that the legislature approved an appropriation for the structure without debate."[187]   Dora also supported construction of a new student union building on the campus of MSU. Stockman's ability to develop disparate consensus is noted in the photographic collection of board members.   Dora was the only woman pictured serving on the board.   All of the political foundation-building led to an even greater opportunity for service in her campaign for the Michigan State Legislature.

---

[187] Darling

7

Along the Campaign Trail
1932-1938

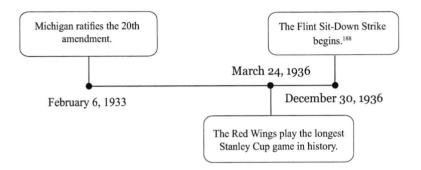

Michigan ratifies the 20th amendment.

The Flint Sit-Down Strike begins.[188]

March 24, 1936

February 6, 1933

December 30, 1936

The Red Wings play the longest Stanley Cup game in history.

While the accomplishments of her life were numerous, it was not yet time to retire from public life. Stockman continued to make advances in her professional life that led her further from the log house, Grange Hall, and college campus to the State Capital of Michigan.

Whether by accident or extremely clever planning, Dora Stockman left the State Board of Control for greener pastures. Initially, it would seem that this would free her to complete the doctoral degree and perhaps resume teaching at the college level. Ill health and widowhood in 1932 were part of the new challenges she faced. However, as a consummate campaigner she embarked on the path that would prepare her to serve in the state legislature. The audience for her message was growing ever wider and she was developing a relationship with the urban setting in the Lansing-East Lansing area. Using

---

[188] *This Date in Michigan History*

her writing skills, she continued to provide music for both the Grange and the wider community. She also became involved in the state taxation committee paving the way for a move to the state capital and never forgetting the base of Grange supporters that propelled her into office.

Departure from the State Board of Control

Local headlines announced Stockman's forthcoming departure from the State Board of Agriculture. One article highlighted her career achievements.

> Mrs. Dora H. Stockman, Michigan's pioneer woman member of the State Board of Agriculture, will leave the chair she held for 12 years on January 1, 1932, after a double term of office characterized by unusual activity

Series of three photographs. *Source: Michigan State University Archives and Historical Collections*
Top: Group photo in front of barn c. 1930's. *Dora-Hall Stockman Collection*
Left: MSU Board of Trustees c. 1930.
Right: MSU Board of Trustees, 1920. *Clark Brody Collection*

as a leader in the field of agriculture.

Perhaps Mrs. Stockman is best known off the campus through her daily broadcasts as the "Sunshine Lady," a regular feature of the WKAR program for two years. Her program consisted of poems and songs for farm children. Much of the material for her feature was drawn from her widely circulated book, *Farmerkins' Farm Rhymes,* some of which have been set to music.

During a long term of office as Grange lecturer in Michigan, Michigan's foremost protagonist of the extension cause was also editor of *The Michigan Patron,* a monthly publication boasting a circulation of 20,000 copies. By virtue of the latter office, she became a member of the Michigan Women's Press Association.[189]

The Stockmans bought a 96-acre farm near Grand Ledge during her second term on the Board of Agriculture where they built yet another home. However, they were not to enjoy this new homestead for long. Two years later, her husband passed away. Francis M. Stockman, Dora's husband of 43 years, passed away in East Lansing on October 23, 1932. He was born on January 20, 1855 in

Dora Stockman with sisters Phoebe and Mina and her brother, Welcome. *Source: the Stockman family.*

---

[189] "Mrs. Dora Stockman Leaves State Board"

Marion, Ohio, and was buried in Hurd Cemetery, northwest of Lansing.[190] Though several years Dora's senior, he provided a supportive environment for Dora to realize her dreams in the field of public service through the Grange and Board of Agriculture.

The following year, 1933, Dora discovered she had diabetes. While health concerns may have slowed her down, she continued to create and in 1934, she wrote the National Grange's prize song, "The Grange Leads on to Victory."

While the doctoral degree in sociology was never completed, she published many excerpts in *The Michigan Patron.* In a public acknowledgment for her efforts on behalf of Michigan State College, Dora was awarded an honorary degree. Surely, she must have been appreciative of the award, as she used the title of doctor in several publications for the next year or so. She shared the podium with a meteorologist in June of 1934. The president of the college was glowing in his praise for her contributions to the Board of Control.

Honorary Doctorate of Law

Stockman received one of two honorary degrees awarded on June 11, 1934. Dr. J. H. Kimball, veteran meteorologist and Stockman received a Doctorate of Law degree from Michigan State College. The degree was to Stockman for her contributions to the college. President Robert Shaw made the following remarks when introducing her at the time of her award:

> Mrs. Dora Hall Stockman, who will receive the degree
> of Doctor of Laws, has been an outstanding figure in

---

[190] D. Stockman, *The Story of Myself*

agricultural education in the State of Michigan; Mrs. Stockman secured her Bachelor of Arts degree in 1899 and her Master's award one year later. She served on the State Board of Agriculture from 1919 through 1931, and was the first woman in the United States to be on the board of control of a land-grant institution.

For many years, Mrs. Stockman was active as Lecturer of the Michigan State Grange, and in educational and legislative programs of that organization. She was also one of the original sponsors of the movement to widen the scope of the College by adding the Liberal Arts course. She has always been an ardent supporter of Agriculture and Home Economics, and was active in obtaining appropriations for the present Home Economics building. Michigan State College owes you a great deal, Mrs. Stockman, and we are proud to confer this honor upon you.[191]

Lyricist, Composer and Arranger

Stockman used the medium open to her, which allowed a platform to voice her opinions. The music that she wrote for the Patrons of Husbandry was yet another avenue to spread the message of hope through participation in Grange Hall activities. The four songbooks contain a wide variety of tunes to which, in many cases, Dora added new words

Michigan State Grange Song Collection. *Source: Author's personal collection.*

---

[191] "Dora H. Stockman Wins High Honors for Self and Grange"

A World Friendship Song

A *World Friendship Song* cover and sheet music. *Source: Michigan State University Archives and Historical Collections.*

to fit her audience. Of the 46 tunes that she created for the song collections, 18 were set to familiar melodies. The songs could educate the young and remind the old of the glories of the nation, God and the Grange. They could be sentimental, patriotic, stirring, or silly. Many of her songs, in which both words and music were composed by Stockman, had a Michigan theme incorporated into them. In the song *Just A Quaint Old Fashioned Farmhouse,* motherhood, family, and education are central. [192]

Support for the family was crucial then as it is now.

Dora increased her activity through public appearance and writing. She published and held the copyright in 1935 for yet another *Michigan State Grange Song Collection,* third edition, as Chairman of the State Grange Home Economic Committee. Stockman sold advertising to underwrite expenses. She included this note of explanation: "This book is distributed free to all Michigan Granges. We wish to express our appreciation to our advertisers who have made this songbook possible. In return I am sure we shall patronize them as they have contributed to our pleasure for the good of all of us."

A publishing house, Eldridge Entertainment House, Inc., out of Franklin, Ohio, advertised the song collection with enthusiasm. The distributor was promoting eight new

---

[192] *Michigan State Grange Song Collection, 5th edition*

entertainment books including *Twenty-Five Peppy Grange Songs and Practical Programs for Grange and Other Rural Groups.* If eight books were not enough, the readers were invited to request a catalog of "Cleanest and Most Clever Secular and Sacred Plays, Pageants, Etc."[193] Another sponsor was the Michigan Milk Producers Association promoting the value of milk: "Nutritional Science backs every claim for their great worth. Use plenty of milk, cream, butter, and cheese. Do not sell it all. Successful milk production depends on good merchandising. Both depend on you helping yourself to Nature's Best Food."[194] Advertisements included items of interest to the agricultural community from the Bureau of Animal Industry, Department of Agriculture, and Lansing, Michigan, promoting State Herds Purebred Holstein Cattle, the Michigan Live Stock Exchange, a fertilizer company, and a poultry farm in Zeeland, Michigan. Other advertising promoted hotels, insurance, monument, school supplies, and the large Reo Motor Car Company located in Lansing, Michigan.

Dora added to the world of music with her song about the state's well-known cherry crop. A note appeared at the bottom of the 1935 sheet music for *Wonderland in Cherryland*: "The above lyrical tribute to Cherryland was written by Mrs. Dora H. Stockman of Lansing, former member of the State Board of Agriculture." Again, the muses called in 1936 and she wrote *World Friendship Song.*

TIME Magazine headlined an article with a phrase from Dora's poem. In June of 1936 that Stockman read a poem she had dedicated to the Associated Country Women of the World which had its third meeting in Washington, D.C. The magazine included the text from the last verse of the poem:

---

[193] *Michigan State Grange Song Collection, 3rd edition*   [194] *Michigan State Grange Song Collection, 3rd edition*

Great God of all the nations,
We come a might throng
With hand clasped hand in greeting
We sing a glorious song.
A prayer for faith and courage,
Peace and friendship's flag unfurled
From the homes of every country,
Country Women of the World![195]

Dora knew how to gather and use publicity. Capitalizing on the *World Friendship Song* written for The Associated County Women of the World meeting in Washington, Stockman described her delight in the meeting for the reporter from the *Grand Rapids Press*. The headline on the following day illustrates her awareness of the media: "Grange Bard Sets Records. Mrs. Dora H. Stockman has slept in more farm beds in Michigan than any other man or woman in the state." The article recounts her many days in service to the Grange beginning in 1908 when she was a platform speaker for farmers' institutes:

> She has spoken in every county in the state dozens and dozens of times. Audiences in virtually every city, village and community in Michigan have listened to her discuss the issues of the day in her own characteristic way. Blessed with a pleasant voice for public speaking, her services have been in great demand at rural and urban meetings in all parts of the state. Mrs. Stockman's audiences have not been limited to Michigan. She has appeared on farmers institute and Grange programs in many states.

---

[195] "Friendship's Flag Unfurled"

While Mrs. Stockman has gained national reputation through her speaking talents and leadership, she is perhaps proudest of her unofficial position as bard of the Michigan State Grange and the National Grange. She gets a poetic delight out of putting her thoughts into rhymes and songs.[196]

While not officially announcing her candidacy for the State House in Lansing, she was working in public forums that provided exposure to a wide range of potential voters. She continued to shore up the base of the electorate that had supported her when she ran successfully for the State Board of Control. Women of the Grange continued to be crucial in the campaign success.

The Michigan Patron

The Michigan Patron Aug-Sept 1934. *Source: State of Michigan Library*

---

[196] Runnells

Dora moved to the role of Advertising Manager in May of 1937 for *The Michigan Patron.* Drawing on the material in her dissertation draft "The Grange and Rural Life in America," Stockman tells the history and background of the Grange. The agricultural newspaper also featured two of her poems: "Grandmothering" and "Mothers of Men." In this issue, she traveled for the Grange and visited Oakland County where she spoke briefly at the Oakland County Pomona Grange."

The June 1937 issue of the *Michigan Patron* included yet another poem entitled "June" and a feature story by Dora on the Grange entitled "The Importance of the State Grange." In July, her poem "Happiness" was included.

More personal appearances are noted in the August 1937 edition. Stockman made an appearance at the Tri-County Picnic at Glen Lake on August 14th at Old Settlers Picnic Grounds. Her featured article is "The Grange and Religion." This time, the poem is "How the Lord Made Michigan."

In the September and October 1937 editions of *The Michigan Patron,* Dora continues to tell the history of the Grange and discusses the decline of the Grange. With honorary doctorate in hand, her byline was now "Dr. Dora H. Stockman" in the November 1937 issue. A portion of the serial story, Chapter III, part 2, of "The Modem Magic Carpet," appears in this issue. The poem in this issue was entitled "Rats." The 1938 issues included more poems and essays by Stockman including "Our Guardian Angels," "We Are the Government," "God Gave to Women," and "A Prayer for Peace." Also included in the paper was an essay, "What I Would Do to Prevent War." The history of the Grange was also continuing in "The Grange in Rural Life in America." This was a vital forum for reaching voters in the campaign for a seat in the State House.

A letter dated August 1, 1938, thanks the voters for signing her petition for the Republican candidacy for state representative. Along with pledging her support, she reminds the voters of her presence on the State Tax Study Commission:

> The fact that I am a member of the present State Tax Study Commission, authorized by the last Legislature, is evidence that I am sharing in helping to try to solve the problems of Equity of Taxation. Our committee has been working for nearly a year on a report to be submitted to the next legislature which will be one of the most important questions to be considered by the 1939 session. This study has equipped me to better understand the taxation system of Michigan, its receipts and expenditures; and to systematize and equalize costs of our government.

Campaign for the State Legislature

Along the campaign trail, Stockman made the following speech that highlights her legislative aims and points out her involvement in the taxation committee before election. Stockman used the contemporary medium of radio to increase her ability to contact voters. A portion of her radio address follows from the first campaign for the House of State House of Representatives,

MAKE AMERICA SAFE FOR THE CHILDREN

By Dora H. Stockman

Hark, America, there's a cry of anguish,
From the mothers in all the land,
Our most precious possessions, the children,
Are being sacrificed on every hand;
Not on superstitious heathen altars,
To satisfy an ancient creed
But the life-blood of the nation is poured out,
In a libation to thoughtless greed.

Make America Safe for the Children poem.
Source: Michigan State University Archives and Historical Collections.

105

November 6, 1938:

> Radio friends, this is Dora H. Stockman, Republican
> Candidate for the State Legislature, of Ingham County,
> second district coming to you over WJIM.

> I come to you this Sunday afternoon because I believe
> that good government is the most important function
> and salvation of any people. Without good government,
> homes, churches, schools, business, and the pursuit of
> happiness languish and perish. America is believed by
> many to be the last stand for Religion, Democracy, and
> Peace....First, for the protection of life and health of our
> citizens, I am now serving on a national health board
> with the objective that every mother and baby may have
> needed care. Michigan has greatly reduced its infant
> mortality rate. I am proud to have had a small part in
> this vital program....

> Second, I have lobbied—yes, lobbied—for equalization
> of school opportunities that all the boys and girls of city
> and country might have a chance to learn not only the
> three R's but to develop skills of hand and brain that
> will also fit them for creative inventions.... Fourth, I
> believe in fair farm prices, adequate wages for labor
> in the cities, reasonable business profits, and hours
> that will leave leisure time for real living. I believe that
> farmers, laborers, and business can prosper at the
> expense of another, but there must be a prosperity for
> all or prosperity for none.

This was a vital source for the campaign that was underway

in 1938 for a seat in the State House. Along the campaign trail, Stockman made the following speech that highlights her legislative aims for education with a portion of a speech on education and taxation. Stockman, not one to overlook new media, gave speeches on the radio.

Speech on Education

Taxpayers these days are questioning (and rightly) where their tax money is being spent, and if they are getting value received for their tax dollars. One big item of tax expenditure is for our public schools. It is a fair question for every citizen to ask, "Are we getting our money's worth for our school tax dollars spent?" Perhaps first of all we would agree that money spent training all the children who are to be the future citizens of the state is not only an ideal long cherished by our state, and every state of our great nation, but an educated citizenry adds to the economic and public welfare of our county.

It is highly significant that perhaps no other function of our government is so near to us as our schools; and that because of this great interest we feel not only free to criticize and evaluate this program which is so vitally connected with the lives of all of our children, but we do want our school dollars to give us our money's worth in economic, health, and cultural values, to our citizens that shall give us the greatest happiness, which is the goal of our democratic government.

It is most important therefore that we evaluate and criticize on the basis of demonstrable facts—and by facts, I do not mean isolated cases, nor facts influenced by personal prejudices. As a person who has been in close contact with schools as a pupil-teacher school administrator, and a mother of three boys, as a keen critic from the viewpoint of Grange leaders, I have kept in constant touch with schools for 50 years.

Now what I have tried to do is not to theorize nor put forward any of my own pet plans or prejudices, but rather to present some real scientific facts as to what schools have done and are doing now for the high majority of our children for the past 20 years. I think I should preface it by stating that looking back into the nineties there were comparatively few college graduates, and the college courses were not as comprehensive nor as practical as our present high school courses.

The era of Public High School did not come in until about 30 years ago. The present high school with its scientifically practical courses is the growth of the past 20 years. The story of the past 20 years of public school education is the marvel of the present age in what it has done and for our children. Is my picture too rosy? Are we satisfied with our schools? By no means. I have a lot of pet schemes to improve them myself. I want to help all the schools to keep going year round. The majority of school plants are mostly idle in summertime. We already have Ag teachers and Home Economic teachers working with students on real farm and home projects in more than 200 schools all summer. We have night classes, short courses, nurseries, and many kinds of out-of-regular-school schools, which are attached to all kinds of government facilities like the W.P.A., N.Y.A., Extension College Services, and believe it or not, these crowded schools are non-compulsory.

With so many taking all this education...of course we get some mediocre and perhaps even cull stuff in a large graduating class. Maybe they cannot all do a job. But, good land, what would they be like without their chance at this educational trough. And some times the really dumb ones like Edison, R.E. Olds, and Ford, Jane Addams, and plenty of others you could mention yourself who just couldn't and didn't have much of a chance in the old school, but took what they could get and what they did with it was plenty. And youth are doing it today in radio, aircraft, research, medicine, and many other fields and there are thousands in our homes, of children in America who just need this chance we can give them in our public schools. They will repay it all back many times in a better citizenry.

Are there lazy teachers? Oh yes, just like some of us other folks. Are there lazy school boards? Yes, indeed. Are there lazy parents? Yes, we know it. Are there many schemes tried out in the name of research? Yes, we know that. Are there high-up dictators who want to keep the status quo, or go back to the good-old-days? Lord help 'em to retire soon. Do our schools need improving? In the good new improved modern English of us all—you bet they do. And thanks for the criticisms that push us to the front to study our needs and faiths. But in spite of all the failings, the schools are the core of our beloved Democracy. We may criticize, chastise, but we love them still. And the money Michigan and America invest in its free schools for its children will keep us a free people.

Dora Stockman was about to use her many skills developed throughout her life as a public speaker, writer, and consensus builder and change agent. She was about to move to the domed capital in Lansing, Michigan to serve the citizens in county or town. Her leitmotif of music and poetry would not be abandoned and her little corner of the world was about to expand even further. For this new endeavor, she would take the memories of childhood from the log house to the state house in support of all state citizens.

The State of Michigan
1938-1945

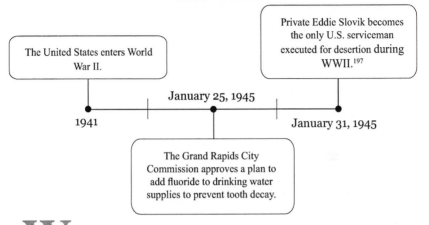

The United States enters World War II.

Private Eddie Slovik becomes the only U.S. serviceman executed for desertion during WWII.[197]

January 25, 1945

1941

January 31, 1945

The Grand Rapids City Commission approves a plan to add fluoride to drinking water supplies to prevent tooth decay.

Wile the accomplishments of her life were numerous, it was not yet time to retire from public life. Dora continued to make sacrifices that led her from the college into the state capital. Throughout Dora Stockman's four terms as a state representative from Michigan, she continued to represent the progressive aims of agriculture. Her legislative contributions continue today in health care insurance reforms, expanded educational opportunity, and liability reforms. She served for four terms as a legislator. This often-overlooked reformer played a vital role in Michigan's history.

At a time when others may plan to retire, Dora, age sixty-six, began the first of four terms in the Michigan State legislature. All of Stockman's campaigning had paid off. Long interested in Republican Party politics, the state office was quickly hers. She became the first Republican woman elected

---

[197] *This Date in Michigan History*

to the state legislature from the 2nd District of Ingham County, now referred to as East Lansing, Michigan. She served on a variety of committees, including the taxation committee that helped frame a law that stopped certain losses for the State on sales taxes already collected. She wrote four amendments that helped pass the milk control bill. Tax law on stocks and bonds and other intangible properties, known as the Stockman Act, raised tax funds that would relieve tax burdens on city and farm real estate. She was first elected in 1938 and re-elected in 1940, 1942, and 1944.

Freshman Legislator

The first primary election showed Dora in a tight race. She

Left: Primary Election Certificate of Nomination. *Source: Michigan State University Archives and Historical Collections.* Right: Campaign Brochure. *Source: Michigan State University Archives and Historical Collections.*

was the only woman on the ballot and defeated three other Republicans in the 2nd district of what is now known as East Lansing, Michigan. Results of the election were noted in *The Michigan Manual.*

1938 Primary Election Results September 13, 1939	
Arthur W. Jewett, Dem	1,673
Walter P. Carven, Rep	2,443
Gary O. Dorlander, Rep	1,283
Dora Stockman, Rep	2,662

With the primary out of the way, she could focus on defeating the remaining Democratic candidate, Arthur W. Jewett. She won by 3,180 votes. Dora was well-known to the college community from her time serving on the Board of Agriculture at Michigan State College.

1938 General Election Results November 8, 1939: Ingham County 2nd District	
Arthur W. Jewett, Democrat	6,446
Dora H. Stockman, Republican	9,626[198]

The general election resulted in two women freshmen legislators in the state of Michigan—Stockman and Ruth Thompson of Muskegon. A newspaper headlined the women's role in the next session of the State House: "Women Legislators

[198] *Michigan Manual*

to Be Seen More Than Heard This Session." The article
described them both.

> Miss Thompson, 51, a comely, gray-haired former
> Muskegon country probate judge, said she came to the
> legislature interested especially in child welfare. Mrs.
> Stockman, 66 years old and a widow, is an active leader
> in the affairs of the Michigan State Grange. She was
> Michigan's first feminine holder of a state office, as a
> member of the state board of agriculture 1920 to 1932.

Stockman wasted no time once she took her seat in the
Michigan State Legislature. In 1939, Stockman introduced
seventeen House Bills. She was placed on several committees
at the start of her legislative career. Committee appointments
included education, general taxation, horticulture, Michigan
School for the Blind, Michigan State College of Agriculture,
and Applied Science.[199]

The Speaker of the House in 1939 directed the Clerk to
read the following benediction written by Representative Dora
Stockman:

> Oh God, Creator and Father of us all,
> We thank thee for our great county.
> We thank thee for Michigan, our own great, glorious
> state.
>
> We thank Thee that it has been our privilege to be the
> official representative charged with the responsibility
> and duty of making laws that will guide, guard and
> protect our own constituents and also with due regard

---

[199] *Michigan House Journal*

to the welfare and prosperity of our whole state of Michigan.

May the Lord bless our efforts for good and forgive our mistakes of omission and commission, as we separate and go to our various homes.

May we truly become bodyguards to uphold and protect the laws of our state, the conservators of our Democracy in word and deed, the guarantors of life, liberty and the pursuit of happiness.

And now, as we separate to go back to our various homes, we pray that the Lord will be with us.

Be behind us to forgive us

Be beside us to defend us

Be before us to guide us

Be above us to bless us to the honor and glory of ourselves and our posterity.

Amen.[200]

Stockman was the leading sponsor of a group medical care bill, the first bill of its kind in the United States. *The Ingham County News* reported on the act in detail: "The purpose of Michigan Medical Service is to assist residents of Michigan in the low income group to obtain the services of doctors of

Building Up Rural Health

How It Is Being Done in Michigan

The Story Interestingly Told By Mrs. Stockman

APPARENTLY the Grange in Michigan is doing pioneer work in behalf of rural health, and it is an interesting story that comes from that wide-awake state. In the report given at Peoria a glimpse was afforded of what is being attempted, but it remains for the facile pen of Dr. Dora H. Stockman to present the complete picture of the Michigan plan, for the benefit of Grange readers everywhere.

hazard when country people have neither the opportunity nor the income to afford needed medical care. The National Grange studied various plans. It investigated the medical systems of nations in the Old World. It studied Canada's hospital and rural care programs. The Grange had a representative on the advisory committee of the U. S. Children's Bureau to study this critical need for better health service. The panel system and state-managed medicine that were prevailing in Europe met with distinct opposition from the

Building Up Rural Health. *Michigan State University Archives and Historical Collections.*

medicine by providing for medical services in return for small monthly subscription payments."[201] Michigan Medical Service evolved into the current Blue Cross/Blue Shield of Michigan. She received a tribute from the Michigan Medical Society at their state convention. Clearly, she was against socialized medicine. She was the leading sponsor of group medical care bill, the first bill in the United States of its kind. The specific House Bill No. 215 is located in the appendix along with several of her contributions to the State of Michigan.

In 1939, Stockman once again used her talents as a poet to prepare a benediction for the Governor. She rose during the Motions and Resolutions portions of the session, March 17, 1939. House Concurrent Resolution No 21 notified that all state department and offices to close until after the funeral, in respect to the family of Governor Frank D. Fitzgerald. Stockman offered the following tribute to the governor:

Michigan is stricken. Her flags are half-mast.
Her Chief has passed into the Great Beyond
Within that open door whose portal never outward swings.
And we are mute with sorrow, bereft of that great leadership
That tireless marched onward and upward with surging,
    battling wings.
Friend of the farmer, he loved the great outdoors
The farm folks who work with God in growing things,
He, a staunch defender of labor, willing to risk his all
That men who work in factories might have their rightful
    heritage
To a living wage—a just reward for toil their labor brings.

---

[201] "Ingham Representative Aided Medical Service"

*And those who guide the destiny of industry listened to his
    counsel*
*That he hoped would bring cooperation, harmony and
    justice,*
*The fruits of democracy for which our nation longs and
    dreams*
And America struggling, thrilling, and visioning sings.
But he has passed within the Open Door and we who stay
Must pick up his challenge and carry on for a better day.
*We must fight to forge the implements of justice that cannot
    fall,*
We must hold wide the gate of golden opportunity for all,
Building the highways of human rights in our fair State
*In monuments kings might envy and only future time can
    estimate.*
*And someday the rugged, fearless, unfinished symphony he
    sung*
*Michigan will carry on to Glory, guardian of the liberties we
    have won.* [202]

In 1939, she drafted concurrent resolution memorializing Congress to prepare an adequate home defense. She served on the taxation committee and helped frame a law that stopped certain losses for the State on Sales Taxes already collected. And she wrote four amendments that helped pass the milk control bill.

Second Term

With her energetic level of accomplishment in her

---

[202] *Michigan House Journal*

freshman term of office completed, she won her second term in office with the following election results reported in *The Michigan Manual*:

Primary election results September 10, 1940 *Ingham County 2nd District*	
Harold J. Harris, Rep	2,194
Dora H. Stockman, Rep	2,925
Ashmon H. Catlin, Dem	1,454

General election results November 5, 1940 *Ingham County 2nd District*	
Dora H. Stockman, Republican	13,551
Ashmon H. Catlin, Democrat	8,357
Leroy Lehman	54
Scattered	1
TOTAL	21,714

Stockman, in her next term of office as State House Representative, sponsored an amusement tax, a bill to finance expansion of vocational education facilities in rural districts, and emergency appropriation for schools showing extreme need. She also served with United States Children's Bureau, National Rural Home Conference, President Hoover's White House Children's Conference, and the Michigan State Educational Advisory Committee; and she attended the Children of Democracy Conference. The following are highlights from Stockman's legislative record.

A few examples of her legislation include authorizing boards

Youth Need Summer School. *Source: Michigan State University Archives and Historical Collections*

of education to borrow money from banking institutions up from estimated revenues for paying current operating deficits [203] and in 1941, she sponsored House Bill 449, a bill to authorize school districts to borrow money and issue bonds for purchase of school buses that was enrolled by the Senate, signed by the Governor, and approved on June 16, 1941 (Public Act No. 220).[204] In that same year, Mrs. Stockman introduced the Appropriation for School for the Blind—$242,000 for new vocational education building; nursery extension building; home economics house and ground improvement. House Bill 314, although failing in the Senate, was introduced Mrs. Stockman, et al. The bill was to increase county library funds by including fines, penalties, etc., now included in county law library funds.[205] She did not abandon her zeal for the Grange, contributing scripts and songs for pageants and meetings. In 1941, Stockman also created a pageant script for Grange Day at Farmer's Week at Michigan State College. She published a play in *The Michigan Patron* called *A Modern Hero.*

Education was also central to Stockman's legislative legacy. As a former teacher, Stockman felt quite strongly about educational issues. According to the Michigan House Journal, Dora Stockman received several educational committee assignments. She sponsored several bills in the house related

---

[203] *Michigan House Journal*

[204] *Michigan House Journal*

[205] *Michigan House Journal*

to the continued strengthening of the school system.

Third Term

Again, in 1942 Stockman was re-elected to State House of Representatives with the following electoral results as reported in *The Michigan Manual*:

Primary Vote for State Rep. September 15, 1942 *Ingham County, Second District*	
Dora H. Stockman, Rep	2,226
Ray E. Whitney, Rep	1,320
Claude Menger, Dem	490

General Election Results November 3, 1942	
Dora H. Stockman, Rep	8,582
Claude Menger, Dem	4,113

Final Term in Office

In 1944, Stockman once again was re-elected to State House of Representatives with the following election results:

Michigan State House of Representatives Primary Election Results July 11, 1944	
Newman J. Blackmore, Rep	279
Frederick Gigax, Rep	555
Dora H. Stockman, Rep	1,572
Ray E. Whitney, Rep	363

General Election Results November 7, 1944	
Dora H. Stockman, Rep	13,736
Scattering	8
TOTAL	13,744

In 1945, she was the chief sponsor of a bill to end monopolies and make Michigan an open state. Stockman was also very interested in dry legislation. She introduced a bill that would take the state out of the liquor business, set a minimum price on liquor, and, according to an undated *Free Press* Lansing Bureau report, do away with drinking places operating outside of municipalities. Stockman is quoted as saying, "I am against the state being in the liquor business. Under the present system the state cannot very well prosecute a department of state and I believe a strong point of this bill is that it would permit prosecution of an individual citizen." Clearly Stockman was displaying frustration in this segment from her response to the question of liquor control.

> In all my legislative experience I have never seen such an indifference to matters that are throughout the State, talked of as much as are conditions on this law. Statements are made everywhere that we never had as bad condition considering women, boys and girls and the easy way they have to acquire habits of drinking than at the present time.[206]

While serving in the Michigan State Legislature, she had the opportunity to address reforms that would help quell the easy

---

[206] "Proposes Open Liquor State"

Drink Cards Required

Measure Asks Costlier Licenses

Free Press Lansing Bureau
906 Prudden Building

LANSING—Long-smouldering dissatisfaction with Michigan liquor control broke out in the Legislature as 12 representatives joined in a bill to end monopoly and make this an open state.

Rep. Dora Stockman, East Lansing, chief sponsor, said that the measure represented her own ideas and not those of organized drys.

Woman Legislator Would End State Liquor Monopoly

By HOWARD J. RUGG
(Journal Staff Writer)

A bill which would take the state out of the liquor business, set a minimum price on liquor, and do away with drinking places operat... to be introduced in the house of representatives Wednesday by Representative Mrs. Dora Stockman, East Lansing Republican.

The bill would eliminate state liquor stores and provide for specially designed "profilers" inste...

Left: Newspaper Article. *Source: Michigan State University Archives and Historical Collections*

Right: Newspaper Article. *Source: Michigan State University Archives and Historical Collections*

access to liquor. House Bill No. 557 called for the elimination of state liquor stores, increases in license fees, and permits for purchases. Introduced by seven other representatives in addition to Mrs. Stockman, the bill was referred to as the Committee on Liquor Traffic.[207]

Again, in 1945, Stockman sponsored another bill on liquor distribution issue and was supported by eleven other members of the House. House Bill No. 19 provided for "liquor; state-stores, abolish; permit importation by individuals; state tax of $1.50 per gallon; minimum price fixed by commission." The bill was referred to the Committee on Liquor Control. [208]

Stockman introduced an additional bill providing for the distribution of funds received from the sale of alcoholic liquor. House Bill No. 230 would allocate the revenue to funding in this manner: 25% to counties, 25% to cities and villages.[209]

Her many prayers and poems and other tributes are noted in the *Journals of the House of Representatives for the State of Michigan*. Many of the other bills never moved out of committee or were turned down by the Senate. She remained in the State

---

[207] *Michigan House Journal*

[208] *Michigan House Journal*

[209] *Michigan House Journal*

Group Photo in front of MSU Union Building. *Michigan State University Archives and Historical Collections*

House for four terms.

The key ideas that she worked on remain unresolved in the State of Michigan. Health care reform with its political and social challenges is very much in the news. Education opportunities are regressing in the areas that Stockman promoted. Legislative support and state dollars for adult and continuing education have been reduced. Liability reform continues to swirl about the capital. Dora sponsored a number of bills to quell the use of alcohol and to enhance the support for higher education and general education as well. Throughout her four terms as a state representative from Michigan, she continued to represent the progressive aims of agriculture. Her legislative contributions continue today in health care insurance reforms, expanded educational opportunity, and liability reforms. This often-overlooked reformer played a vital role in Michigan's history.

123

9

Retirement: A New Beginning
1946-1948

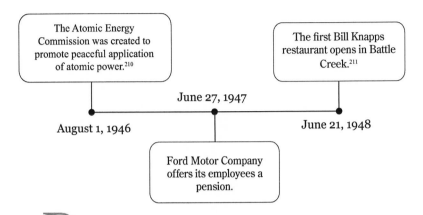

The Atomic Energy Commission was created to promote peaceful application of atomic power.[210]

The first Bill Knapps restaurant opens in Battle Creek.[211]

June 27, 1947

August 1, 1946

June 21, 1948

Ford Motor Company offers its employees a pension.

Dora Stockman was elected to public office as a State Representative four times from the East Lansing, Ingham County area. She sponsored a number of bills to quell the use of alcohol and to enhance the support for higher education and general education as well. She retired from public life in 1946, at the age of seventy-three, sending word of her retirement from St. Petersburg, Florida. At that time, her Ingham County, Michigan address was at 555 East Grand River. As part of her announcement, she endorsed Jacob Schepers of 355 Hillcrest, E. Lansing.

Reflections

Stockman used the medium open to her, which allowed a platform to voice her opinions. In spite of her emphasis

---

[210] "United States and American History: 1946"   [211] *This Date in Michigan History*

supporting the farm family, Stockman's life presented contradictions, for she was absent a great deal of time in order to speak on behalf of those farm families. Her own discouraging views on farming were based on a family history that often encountered hardship. Yet optimism prevailed.

Motherhood, family, and education were important for Stockman. At the edge of the twenty-first century, family values and education are seen as the hope to save the fractured social structures. The lessons of yesterday remain important today. The legacy of the Grange and the plays of Stockman should not be forgotten. Her themes provide an opportunity to learn from the past in order to fashion a way of being for the future.

The shift or structural transformation of American values from small town 1880s to a new bureaucratic minded middle-class by 1920 represented a dramatic change. She would be pleased to learn that the legacy of the Clover Leaf clubs, now 4-H clubs, abound in rural and urban settings. In addition, connections to the Grange are found online as well. Several Grange Halls remain active in Michigan. Stockman's lyrics from "Wonderland in Cherry Land in Michigan" linger at the Traverse City Cherry Festival. Stockman lived a life of a good Granger. She should be remembered.

She was a very frugal individual and the family never had a great deal of disposable income until the farm was sold and her youngest son was ready for college. The family had a summer home in Glen Arbor. She did not care for fancy dress and lived a simple personal life. She seemed to echo the founding principles of the Grange Movement in her exemplary life. Her unpublished autobiography ends with her aims in life being "to strive to make our best contribution to help make our niches of the world a little happier and a little better than when we found

it."

It is striking that the issues raised in the political concerns and considerations as a result of the transformational shift are problems still wrestled with today. Small level political groups, while trying to maintain their island community, are impacted by the larger controlling agencies or legislative bodies. Moreover, local political groups continue to appeal to the grass roots voters in small communities.

Among the legacies of the Grange is the cooperative extension service that once promised to be the route of change for farmers. However, even that is under question. The comments continued on to discuss negative consequences of this delivery model to present-day industry.

A decrease in the size of the farm family is related to the increase in large commercial farming. The rural community has expanded, however, with small towns increasingly drawing from both the farm and larger cities. But, in spite of movements to retain the family farm, the successful agricultural innovations have worked against the farm family in favor of the large corporate farm and niche farm markets.

Stockman discovered a need for change in her pioneering work for the Grange. She established herself as a change agent by participating within the sphere available to a woman of her time. The dialogues of the plays give credence to her recognition of the problem of migration to the cities. She further clarified the problems of the youth on farms in the dialogues of the *Happy Valley* play. Stockman acted as a change agent influencing the lives of those who read, performed, and viewed her plays. The legacy of plays within the Grange movement was a recognized vehicle to entertain and to educate; it was her goal to provide a wholesome environment in *Happy Valley* and elsewhere.

Woman Lawmaker Decides to Retire

Woman Lawmaker Decides to Retire. *Source: Michigan State University Archives and Historical Collections.*

Stereotyping of rural life has been a popular sport since earliest recorded time. The poor country bumpkin in American playwriting became a theatrical cliché, as did the Yankee character. There is a need to exercise care when judging a work of the rural writer Stockman. The motives for creating plays for a rural audience stemmed from a certainty about the goals for the Patrons of Husbandry.

Throughout her life, Stockman retained a missionary zeal for her task of awakening the rural family. She followed her plan to make her corner of the world a little better than it was before. Stockman's life illustrates a determination to create, participate, and motivate.

She was a loyal soldier among the fraternal order that highlighted so much of her life. Stockman was a trailblazer whose mission should no longer be held secret. Her contributions are a part of the ongoing history of this nation. Her story is compelling and worth sharing, and works against the myth of the poor country cousin.

In contemporary circumstances through technological advances, it may once more be possible to imagine a life of rural and urban isolation. The foundation of Stockman's writing may reinforce the ability to remain part of a social circle while working in relative isolation at home with present day technology.

Over a hundred years ago, the Grange founders created a blueprint for the new community organization through a central vehicle, the Grange Hall. As a change agent, Stockman contributed an enduring legacy. The author's hope is to contribute to the rich harvest provided by contemporary women's studies of new knowledge about women's contribution for the life of this nation.

Remarriage

Politics set aside, Dora was ready for yet another adventure. According to family members, she was a great fan of the Rose Bowl and had attended many college football bowl games in Pasadena. That is, according to a family member, where she met her future husband, Gustof Weinkauf, of Grass Lake, Michigan. She remarried in April of 1947.

According to her son, she arrived one day for a visit and surprised him by saying, "Son, I'd like you to meet your Dad." The shock was understandable. Dora, it seems, had been acquainted with Mr. Weinkauf through a connection with the Rose Bowl games. The marriage, however, was not one that lasted very long, because in 1948, while in Berkley, California at the age of seventy-six after an illness of less than a week, she died. Located in the archives is a wire service report of her death. "She died in California after an illness of less than a week. Her body will be returned here Sunday for funeral services next week."[212] Her body was interred at Hurd Cemetery next to her partner of long duration, Francis, her first husband, under a Grange headstone.

---

[212] Darling

Former Woman Lawmaker, Ex-Grange Officer Dies

LANSING – (P) – Word was received here today of the death Tuesday at the age of 75 of Mrs. Doar H. Stockman Weinkauf, author, former Republican legislator and State Grange lecturer.

Her long career of public serv-

Born in a log cabin at Marilla, Manistee County, Aug. 4, 1872, Mrs. Weinkauf received her education in the public schools of Marilla Township, Benzonia College and Hillsdale College. She received a master of arts degree

Former Woman Lawmaker, Ex-Grange Officer Dies. *Source: Michigan State University Archives and Historical Collections*

Dora Hall Stockman. *Source: author's personal collection*

Epilogue

Michigan State University waited a number of years after her death before publicly acknowledging her contributions to the MSU and the State of Michigan. In 1987, the campus newspaper featured a story on the dedication of a memorial marker on the triangle in front of Agriculture Hall. In 2000 a State of Michigan historical at Kalamazoo is dedicated to Women in the Michigan Grange. Dora is noted for her clover club and elective offices. In 2006, Stockman was inducted into the historical category by the Michigan Women's Hall of Fame.

Moreover, what of other changes brought about by Stockman? The Juvenile Grange continues with a change of name from Clover clubs to 4-H clubs, but they continue to flourish in rural areas and in urban settings as well. The progressive reforms in education are still unfolding. Only recently school districts have begun to experiment with a year-round program. Taxation on entertainment continues to be topical with the public media discussion of support for stadium building. In the area of liquor control, the State of Michigan only recently got out of the liquor control business that Stockman had suggested in the 40s. Public health care continues to be under scrutiny for both urban and rural families.

Stockman advanced the cause of the progressive era and the family in particular. She was a good Granger through and through. The Stockman family headstone is a granger-sponsored stone with the sheaves of wheat strongly etched. She indeed had made life a little sweeter for her presence. The story of her ambitious work with the Grange, Michigan Agricultural College, and the House of Representatives provides a glimpse of an era and appreciation of an enterprising progressive rural woman clearly ahead of her time. Stockman was a remarkable, pioneering woman who should not be forgotten in the history of Michigan women.

Appendices

Timeline

1872: Born in a log house in Marilla Township, Manistee County, Michigan

1874: Parents, Leander F. and Lucy J. Hall, join the Grange

1886: Passed the teacher exam at age 14

1888: Begins teaching at age 16

1888: Meets future husband, Francis, at religious revival service

1889: Married, Francis M. Stockman, brings two children and widowed mother

1890: Mother-in-law dies

1890: Older stepson dies of malignant diphtheria

1891: Sold farm to begin mercantile business in Arcadia

1892: First son, Lee, born

1895: Family moves to Benzonia to run a department store.

1895-1902: Literary course and Master's Degree

1902: Brief move to Oregon for husband's health.

1902: Returns to Michigan to help ailing mother

1902: Begins teaching and study at Hillsdale College

1903: Receives degree from Hillsdale College-serves as class secretary

1903: Husband returns. Grand River Farm near of Lansing is purchased

1905: Daughter, Lucy born and dies 6 days later of spina bifida.

1906: Sells first long story "The Price of a Farm" to The Michigan Farmer

1907: Second son, Verne, born

1910: H.R. Pattengill publish Book of Dialogs

1911: Farmikins Farm Rhymes book of verse published

1913: Appointed by Gov. Ferris to attend international Congress of Farm Women

1914: Elected State Grange Lecturer. Served until 1930.

1916: The Coming of Happy Valley Grange to Hard Scrabble Hollow presented.

1919: Elected to State Board of Agriculture. Serves two terms for 12 years.

1925: Sells off cattle and moves to East Lansing.

1930: Begins doctoral work in sociology at Michigan State College

1932: Becomes widow

1934: Awarded honorary Doctorate of Law Degree by Michigan State.

1935: Composes "Wonderland in Cherryland"

1937: Runs for Grange Master position.

1938: Elected to Michigan legislature from Ingham County's 2nd district.

1940-1944: Reelected three more times as State House Representative.

1946: Retires from politics, age 74.

1947: Remarries Gustof Weinkauf of Grass Lake, Michigan. Moves to Berkley, California

1948: Dies in California, on May 27 age 76. Buried near her first husband in Lansing.

Selected Plays and Stories by Dora Stockman

A Master Stroke
A Modern Hero
A Patriotic Party
An Old Fashioned Mother
Blossom's Letter to Santa Clause
Brownies and Fairies on a Strike
Dr. Mary's Prescription
Hero Worshipers
Neenah's Gratitude
Santa Claus Visits the Williams Family
Santa Clause Junior Substitute
The Golden Wedding
The Coming of Happy Valley Grange to Hard Scrabble Hollow
The Hope of Israel
The Imprisoned Princess
The Old and the New Santa Claus
The Report of the Thanksgiving Dinner Committee

Selected Poems of Dora Stockman

"A Mother's Work"
"Farm Firesides"
"Glorifying the Common Day"
"God's Color Symphony"
"Make America Safe for the Children"
"Michigan's Northland Autumn Beauty"
"My Dream of Home"
"That Bothersome Boy"
"The Farmer's Compensation"
"The House of Happiness"
"The Quilt"
"Three Pioneers of Michigan"
"When the Blue Star Turned to Gold"

Stockman Lyrics & Music

"An Apple Blossom Song"

"Banish Tyrant Cigaret"—Tune "Yankee Doodle"

"Benediction"

"The Bird for the Farmer"—Tune "Marching Through
    Georgia"

"By The Fireside I'm Dreaming Tonight"

"Fill The Hours With Joy Today"—Tune "Silver Threads
Among the Gold"

"God of the Nations, Give Us Peace"

"Good Night, Good Bye"

"Grange Alma Mater"—Tune: Old College Tune Grange
Closing

"Ode"—Tune: Old Hundredth-The Doxology

"The Grange Creed"

"Grange Golden Sheaf and Silver Star"—Tune: The Farmer in
    the Dell

"Grange Opening Ode"—Tune: America

"The Grange is Marching On"—Tune: "Tramp, Tramp,
    Tramp"

"The Grange Leads On To Victory"—Tune: Verne A.
    Stockman

"I'm Going Back to Our Old Homestead"

"Hail to the Flag"

"Indian Mich-i-gan"

"Just a Quaint Old-Fashioned Farmhouse"

"Land of Delight, My Michigan"

"The Last Long Furrow"—Tune: "Old Folks at Home"

"Lord Let Me Lean On You"

"The Love That Shines in Mother's Eyes"—Tune: "Alohe"

"Lullaby"—Tune: "Long, Long Ago"

"Michigan Indian Song"

"My Flag and Your Flag"—Tune: Verne A. Stockman & Goldie Palmer Brooks

"Oh! Land of Mine"

"Oh State of Mine, My Michigan"

"Oh, We Love to Sing They Story, Michigan"—Tune: "Illinois" by Ch. Chamberlain

"An Old-Fashioned Locket"

"Onward Marching"

"Our Flag For A Thousand Years"—Tune: "Song of a Thousand Years"

"Roses"—Tune: Verne A. Stockman

"Sell Off That Brindle Breed"—Tune "Mary Had a Little Lamb"

"A Singing Grace"

"Sing the Glory of the Grange"

"Song Of The Hen"

"There's A Homestead In The Country"—Tune "Comin' Thro' the Rye"

"The State I Love to Live In"—Tune: "Dixie"

"A Weaving Song"

"We Sing to Grange Colors"—Tune: Old College Tune

"When I Pray"

"When The Last Long Furrow Is Ended"—Tune: "Swanee River"

"A World Friendship Song"—Piano Arr. by: C. Byron Morton

"Wonderland In Cherryland In Michigan"

"Youthful Heralds"

Legislative Highlights

1938 Primary Election Results	
Arthur W. Jewett, Democrat	1,673
Walter P. Carven, Republican	2,443
Gary O. Dorlander, Republican	1,283
Dora Stockman, Republican	2,662

1938 General Election Results Ingham County 2nd District	
Arthur W. Jewett, Democrat	6,446
Dora Stockman, Republican	9,626
Scattering	5[213]

In 1939, Mrs. Stockman introduced seventeen House Bills according to the general index to the House Journal, 1939, vol. 2, p 2315.

1939 Michigan House Journal

Committee Appointments for Mrs. Stockman: Education, General Taxation, Horticulture, Michigan School for the Blind, Michigan State College of Agriculture and Applied Science

The Speaker directed the Clerk to read the following benediction written by Representative Dora Stockman.

House Bill No. 84. A bill to appropriate $9,000,000 from the

---

[213] *Michigan Manual 1938*

general fund for use by distressed schools during the next five months introduced by Mrs. Stockman and referred to the Committee on Ways and Means.

House Bill No. 135. A bill asking Governor to convey to the state board of agriculture certain lands in Ingham county. Mrs. Stockman and Mr. Gilbert introduced the bill. It was referred to the Committee on Agriculture, approved by the Senate and approved by the Governor becoming Public Act No. 74.

House Bill No. 180 introduced by Mrs. Stockman. A bill to create a special school emergency fund for the remainder of current fiscal year and appropriation of $500,000 thereto. The bill was referred to the Committee on Ways and Means and died in the Senate.

House Bill No. 181 introduced by Mrs. Stockman to make appropriations for support during the next two fiscal years. The bill was referred to the Committee on Education and then to the Committee on Ways and Means.

House Bill No. 215. Bill to regulate incorporation of non-profit medical care corporations, introduced by Mrs. Stockman, et al. Referred to the Committee on Public Health, referred to Senate, approved by Governor. It became Public Act No. 108.

During the Motions and Resolutions portions of the session, March 17, 1939, House Concurrent Resolution No. 21 notified all state department and offices to close until after the funeral, in respect to the family of Governor Frank D. Fitzgerald. Mrs. Stockman rose to a question of personal privilege and offered the following tribute to the governor.

Michigan is stricken. Her flags are half-mast.

Her Chief has passed into the Great Beyond...

Michigan will carry on to Glory, guardian of the liberties we have

won.

House Bill No. 351. A bill to amend section 27 of chapter 2 of part 2 of Act No 319 of the Public Acts of 192—authorizes boards of education to borrow money from banking institutions up to June 30, 1940—a certain amount from estimated revenues for paying current operating deficits. Introduced by Mrs. Stockman, et al., amended in the Senate, approved by Acting Governor.

Mr. Kircher and Mrs. Stockman introduced House Bill No. 442. A bill to amend section 3 of Act No. 320 of the Public Act of 1927, entitled as amended "An act authorizing counties, cities and villages, either individually or jointly by agreement, to provide a sanitary means of disposing of the garbage, sewage and night soil thereof; to charge owners or occupants of premises thereof; to borrow money and issue bonds to own, acquire, construct, equip, operate and maintain intercepting sewers and sewage disposal plants, and garbage disposal plant, and to repeal Act No. 2 of the Extra Session of 1926, and any other acts or parts of acts inconsistent herewith," as amended being section 2468 of the Compiled Laws of 1929. Referred to the Committee on Towns and Counties.

House Bill No. 445. A bill to prevent hunting for game on Sunday, in the county of Ingham.; to authorize the arrest of persons violating the provisions of this act; to prescribe penalty thereof; and to provide a referendum thereon. Mrs. Stockman and Mr. Kircher introduced bill that was referred to the Committee on Conservation.

House Bill No. 471. Requires licensing of tourist homes and cabins, etc. Introduced by Mrs. Stockman and Miss Thompson, to be known as the "Dora-Ruth Bill." Died in the Senate.

House Bill No. 473. Provides for appropriation for medical and surgical treatment of Fred W. DeClaire. Introduced by Mrs. Stockman. Referred to the Committee on Ways and Means.

House Bill No. 508. To amend Section 7 of Chapter 81 of the Revised Statutes of 1816-Bill of sale for goods and chattels involving transfer of ownership to be accompanied by certificate as to county personal taxes when presented to register of deeds for filing. Introduced by Mrs. Stockman and referred to the Committee on Judiciary.

House Bill No. 528. Provides for specific tax upon the ownership of intangible personal property. Introduced by Mrs. Stockman and seven other reps. Referred to the Committee on General Taxation.

House Bill No. 549. To amend Section 1 of Act No. 154, P.A. 1915—Provides that milk or cream may be sold in bottles or jars of capacity of one gallon. Introduced by Mr. Braun and Mrs. Stockman, died in the Senate.

House Bill No. 557. To amend title and sections 2,3,6,14,15,16, 19 and 24 of Act No. 8, P.A. Extra Session 1933—Elimination of state liquor stores; increases license fees, permits for purchases, etc. Introduced by seven other reps in addition to Mrs. Stockman. Referred to the Committee on Liquor Traffic.

House Bill No. 606. Authorizes township boards to transfer to county park trustees management of lands held for park purposes. Introduced by Mr. Kircher and Mrs. Stockman, approved by the Senate, signed by the Governor. It became Public Act No. 300.

1939-1940 Sixtieth Legislature Seat and Committee assignments. Seat 35. Education, General Taxation, Horticulture, Michigan School for the Blind, Michigan State College of Agriculture and Applied Science, Religious and Benevolent Societies.

1941-1942 General election results November 5, 1940 Ingham County 2nd District	
Dora H. Stockman, Republican	13,551
Ashmon H. Catlin , Democrat	8,357
Leroy Lehman	54
Scott	12[214]

1941 Michigan House Journal Vol. 2

In 1941 Mrs. Stockman introduced nineteen bills. According to the 1941 Michigan House Journal, she offered the invocation three times.

House Bill 232 amended section 1 of Act No. 113, P.A.

---

[214] *Michigan Manual*

1935—Increases mill tax for Michigan State College and limits appropriation to $2,950,000.00. Mrs. Stockman, together with five other house members, introduced the bill that eventually became a joint resolution and was presented to the Governor for approval on June 19, 1941 (Public Act No. 358)

In that same year, Mrs. Stockman introduced the Appropriation for School for the Blind—$ 242,000 for new vocational education building; nursery extension building; home economics house and ground improvement.

House Bill 314 died in the Senate, was introduced Mrs. Stockman, et al. The bill was to increase county library funds by including fines, penalties, etc., now included in county law library funds.

House Bill 448 introduced an appropriation of $5,000,000 for aid in school district building construction program. Mrs. Stockman jointly introduced the bill that was referred to the Committee on Ways and Means.

House Bill 449 followed, introducing an amendment to section 1 of chapter 12 of part 2 of Act No. 319, P.A. 1927—Authorizes school districts to borrow money and issue bonds for purchase of school buses. This bill was enrolled by the Senate, signed by the Governor and approved, June 16, 1941 (Public Act No. 220).

House Bill 484 provides for tax on admissions to places of amusement. Introduced by Mrs. Stockman, et al., referred to Committee on State Affairs.

House Bill 553 sinking funds for purchase of sites and construction and repair of school buildings—authorizes 5 mill tax for 5 year period. Majority vote of school electors required. Introduced by Mrs. Stockman, et al. Became Public Act No. 223.

"Mrs. Stockman having reserved the right to explain her vote upon the passage of the bill, made the following statement: 'Mr. Speaker and Members of the House: I am casting my vote for House Bill No. 562, not from a farm standpoint but at the request of scores of workers from Flint, Detroit, Muskegon and Lansing who say 'we want the right to vote whether we shall strike or not, uncoerced'" (May 22, 1941. No. 92, p 1520).

Primary Vote for State Rep. September 15, 1942 Ingham County, Second District	
Dora H. Stockman, Rep	2,226
Ray E. Whitney, Rep	1,320
Claude Menger, Dem	490

General Election Results	
Dora H. Stockman, Rep	8,582
Claude Menger, Dem	4,113 [215]

The Michigan Manual, official Directory and Legislative Manual published by the State of Michigan 1943-1944, describes Dora H. Stockman's occupation as lecturer and writer. Her

[215] *Michigan Manual*

145

committee assignments were in education, Girls' Training School, Michigan School for the Blind, Michigan State College of Agriculture and Applied Science and Public Health.

1943 History of House Bills

House Bill 1. To amend the title and section 1 of Act No. 5. P.A. 1885—Time Bill, to establish standards of time in the state of Michigan, subject to local option of legislative bodies of municipalities, limited to duration of public law 403 of the 77th Congress. Mrs. Stockman was the second person named as introducing this bill that resulted in Senate approval and the signature of the Governor. It became Public Act No. 1 (1943, p 1345).

House Bill 3. To amend section 10 of Act No. 123, P.A. 1893—School for the Blind clothing and necessary expense for destitute blind to be paid from school fund instead of general fund. This was referred to the Committee on Ways and Means (1943, p 1345).

House Bill 77. Appropriation of $2,000,000.00 for purchase of land west of present state office building for addition to office building. Fifty-eight reps introduced this bill. Mrs. Stockman was among them. The bill was referred to the Committee on Ways and Means (1943, 1359).

House Bill 224. To amend section 3 of chapter 5 of part 1, Act No 319, P.A. 1927—Schools, rural agricultural, amend section providing for by consolidation, in regards to valuation, petitions, etc.; prohibit district board of township school district from forming without petition to county commissioner of schools. Introduced by Mrs. Stockman and referred to the Committee on Education (1943, p 1387).

House Bill 235. To amend Act No. 328, P.A. 1931—Rabbits, fowl or poultry, inhuman treatment of, make misdemeanor. Introduced by Rep. Stockman and referred to the Committee on Judiciary (1943, p 1390).

House Bill 256. To amend Act No. 328, P.A. 1931—Livestock, transportation of in manner to endanger life or limb, or of different kinds or sizes without separation partitions, made misdemeanor. Introduced by Rep. Stockman and referred to the Committee on Judiciary (1943, p 1394).

House Bill 264. To amend section 11 of Act No. 1009, P.A. 1939—Hospital service insurance, alternate care method, authorizes if hospital space unavailable. Introduced by Rep. Stockman., approved by Senate, signed by Governor became Public Act No. 229 (1943, p 1396).

House Bill 403. To amend section 1, Act No. 302 P.A. 1927—Education, county supervisors of, require, in counties having 60 but less than 120 rural teachers and 2 in counties with more than 120 rural teachers. Introduced by Rep. Stockman and referred to the Committee on Education (1943, p 1420).

1943 Michigan House Journal

The Hon. Dora H. Stockman, Representative from Ingham County, offered the invocation at the opening of session number forty-seven, March 16, 1943.

Journals of the Senate and House of Representatives Second Extra Session of 1944

The Speaker filed written notice with the Clerk that he had named Representative Stockman as Acting Speaker for Tuesday, June 20, 1944.

From the Journals of the Senate and House of Representative Extra Session of 1946

House Bill 23. Adult education; permit program on county basis by board of supervisors under supervision of superintendent of public instruction. Mrs. Stockman one of the nine reps introducing the bill. That was approved by the Senate, signed by the Governor becoming Public Act No. 18.

1945 Michigan House Journal

House Bill No. 19. To amend the title and sections 2, 3, 6, 14, 17, 19, and 24 of Act No 8, P.A. 1933, Extra Sessions—Liquor; state-stores, abolish; permit importation by individuals; state tax of $1.50 per gallon; minimum price fixed by commission, etc. introduced by Mrs. Stockman and 11 other reps. Bill referred to Committee on Liquor Control.

House Bill No. 72. To amend sections 2 and 15 of chapter 4 of part 1 of Act No. 319, P.A. 1927—Schools, third class, voting on township district, permit; increase population basis from 3,000 to 25,000. Introduced by Rep. Stockman. Approved by the Senate and Governor becoming Public Act No. 171.

House Bill No. 187. To amend sections 2,3,4,5,6,7,8,14 and 15 of Act No. 297. P.A. 1937 and to repeal sections 9,10,11 and 12 of Act No 297, P.A. 1937—Soil conservation districts law, amend as declaration of policy; formation of conservation committee; compensation and expense of committee; boundary changes; district officers; acceptance of gifts, etc. Mrs. Stockman was among the five reps co-sponsoring the bill that was approved by the Senate and Governor becoming Public Act No. 280.

House Bill No. 201. Imposes an excise and specific tax on cigarettes; regulates and licenses manufacturers, wholesalers, distributors and retailers; prescribes rules and regulations and distribution of proceeds. Introduced by Mrs. Stockman and six other reps. Referred to the Committee on General Taxation.

House Bill No. 202. To amend Act No. 8, P.A. 1933. Extra-session—Provides for tax of 6% of the sales price on all alcoholic liquor. Introduced by Mrs. Stockman and six other reps. Referred to the Committee on General Taxation.

House Bill No. 230. To amend section 49 of Act No. 8, P.A. 1933, Extra Session—
Distribution of moneys derived from sale of alcoholic liquor, 25% to counties, 25% to cities and villages. Introduced by Mrs. Stockman and six additional reps. Referred to Committee on State Affairs.

House Bill No. 240. To amend chapter 3 part 2 of Act No 319, P.A. 1927—School districts, creates county reorganization committee; prescribes powers and duties (study committee). Introduced by six reps including Mrs. Stockman. Died in Senate.

House Bill No. 241. To amend section 3 of chapter 18 of part 2 of Act No. 319, P.A. 1927—Permits 13th and 14th grades as part of public school system. Mrs. Stockman was one of six reps introducing bill that did not make it out of the House.

House Bill No. 242. To amend Act No. 319, P.A. 1927— Provides for organization of fourth class school districts. Introduced by six reps including Mrs. Stockman. Reported on general orders.

House Bill No. 410. To amend section 5 of chapter 17 of Act No. 316, P.A. 1923—
Suspends section of drain law prohibiting pollution of country or intercounty drains for war during and one year. Mrs. Stockman was among three co-sponsors. Bill died in the Senate.

Works Cited

Conservatory Recital Program. Benzonia, MI, 1900.

Hillsdale College Commencement Excercises Program. Hillsdale College, 1903.

History of Manistee County, Michigan. Chicago: H.R. Page & Co, 1882.

The Manistee County Directory. Benzonia: Benzonia Library, 1882.

The Michigan Patron February 1927: cover.

The Michigan Patron (1937).

The Manistee Democrat 1889.

"A Fascinating Michigan Story: How a College Group of Young People Were Set at Work and the Good Results Achieved." National Grange Monthly September 1928: 36.

Addams, Jane. The Spirit of Youth and the City Streets. New York: MacMillan, 1912.

—. Twenty Years at Hull House: With Autobiographical Notes. New York: MacMillan, 1938.

Almond, Gabriel A. Crisis, Choice and Change: Historical Studies of Political Development. Boston: Little Brown & Co., 1973.

"Amusement Ticket Tax Will Be Asked." 1941.

Arcadia Township Board Records 1880-1980. Arcadia, MI, 1980.

Arthur, Elizabeth L. Special Grange Drills and Marches. Syracuse, 1933.

Barns, W.D. Revisionist Historiography and the Patrons of Husbandry. 1979.

"Bay View Assembly." Bay View Bulletin May 1915: 8.

Belasco, David. The Theatre Through Its Stage Door. New York: Harper, 1919.

Bently, Eric, ed. The Theory of the Modern Stage. New York: Penguin Books, 1986.

Blauch, L.E. "Professional Education." Encyclopedia Americana. 1965. 632.

Brockett, Oscar G. Century of Innovation: A History of European and American Theatre and Drama Since 1870. Englewood Cliffs, NJ: Prentice Hall, 1973.

Bromfield, Louis. The Farm. 1946.

—. The Farm: 1896-1956. 1993.

Buck, Solon J. Grange Movement: A Study of Agriculture Organizations and its Political, Economic and Social Meaning 1870-1880. Boston: Harvard University Press, 1984.

Buell, Jennie. One Woman's Work for Farm Women: The Story of Mary A. Mayo's Part in Rural Social Movements. Boston: Whitcomb & Barrows, 1908.

—. The Grange Master and the Grange Lecturer. 1921.

Carlson, Robert A. "Cooperative Extension: An Historical Assessment." Journal Extension (1970): 8.

Carstensen, V. Farmers Discontent: 1865-1900. New York: Wiley & Sons, 1974.

Case, Herbert, ed. The Official Who's Who in Michigan. Munising, 1936.

Catton, Bruce. Waiting for the Morning Train. New York: Doubleday & Co., 1972.

"Certainly a Well Balanced Grange in Michigan." National Grange Monthly October 1945.

"Chronology of Michigan Women's History." Michigan Women's Historical Center. 2 January 2007 <http://www.michiganwomenshalloffame.org/pages/timeline.htm>.

Conway, Robert J. The Woman in America. Ed. R.J. Lifton. Boston: Beacon Press, 1967.

Darling, B. "From Lansing Past...A Profile of Dora Stockman: Woman of Many Talents." The State Journal 29 May 1960: 22. deTocqueville, Alexis. Democracy in America. Ed. 1963 Richard D. Heffner. New York: The New American Library, 1840.

"Dora H. Stockman Wins High Honors For Self & Grange." The Michigan Patron August-September 1934: 1.

"Drink Cards Required." Detroit Free Press 1945.

Eckey, Lorelei and et al. 1,001 Broadways: Hometown Talent on Stage. Ames, Iowa: Iowa State University, 1982.

Erikson, E. The Woman in America. Ed. R.J. Lifton. Boston: Beacon Press, 1967.

"Extention Division." State Board of Agriculture Report. 1927.

Fink, Deborah. Agrarian Women: Wives and Mothers in Rural Nebraska 1880-1940. Chapel Hill: University of North Carolina Press, 1992.

—. Open Country Iowa: Rural Women. Tradition and Change. New York:

State University of New York Press, 1986.

Flint, W. "Rural Poverty in America." Phi Kappa Phi Journal (1996): 76.

Franck, Irene and David S. Brownstone. Women's World: A Timeline of Women in History. New York: Harper Collins, 1995.

"Friendship's Flag Unfurled." TIME Magazine. 15 June 1936 <http://www.time.com/time/magazine/article/0,9171,756283,00.html>

Gard, Robert E. and G.S. Burley. Community Theatre: Idea and Achievement. New York: Duell, Sloan and Pearche, 1959.

Gard, Robert E. Grassroots Theatre: A Search for Regional Arts in America. Madison: University of Wisconsin, 1995.

Gard, Robert E., M. Balkch and P.B. Temkin. Theatre in America: Appraisal and Challenge. New York: Theatre Arts Books, 1968.

Gardner, Charles M. "Helping Young People to Help Themselves—The Grange Method and Its Results." Education May 1921: 588-598.

—. The Grange—Friend of the Farmer. Washington D.C.: The National Grange, 1949.

Godkin, Edwin. L. (1876) "The Grange Collapse." The Nation. New York: NY. Jan 27. 57

Grange, Michigan State. "Dora H. Stockman Wins High Honors for Self & Grange." The Michigan Patron August-September 1934: 1.

Greer, Thomas H. American Social Reform Movements: Their Pattern Since 1865. Port Washington: Kennikat Press, 1965.

Grimsted, David. Melodrama Unveiled: American Theatre and Culture 1800-1850. Los Angeles: University of California Press, 1968.

Grose, B. Donald and Franklin O. Kenworthy. A Mirror of Life: A History of Western Theater. New York: Holt Rinehart & Winston, 1985.

Grun, Bernard. The Timetables of History. New York: Simon & Schuster, 1979.

Gurko, Miriam. The Ladies of Seneca Falls: The Birth of the Woman's Rights Movement. New York: Schocken Books, 1974.

Hilliard, Evelyne. Amateur and Educational Dramatics. New York: MacMillan, 1917.

Hodysch, H.W. "Objectivity and History in the Study of Higher Education: A Note on the Methodology of Research." Canadian Journal of Higher Education (1987): 17.

Holbrook, Stewart. Down on the Farm: A Picture Treasury of Country

Life in Good Old Days. New York: Bonanza Books, 1954.

Holden, E.A., ed. Souvenir: National Grange in Lansing, MI. Lansing: R. Smith, 1902.

Holland, Sarah Fisher. Grange Drill Manual. Boston: Boston Press, 1926.

Horton, Guy B. History of the Grange in Vermont. Montpelier, Vermont, 1926.

Hoyt, Harlowe Randall. Town Hall Tonight. New York: Prentice Hall, 1955.

"Ingham Representative Aided Medical Service ." Ingham County News No. 16 1939.

"Ingham's Lady Lawmaker Gets Long-Coveted House Seat 100." Ingham County News

Jensen, J.M. "You May Depend She Does Not Eat Much Idle Bread: Mid-Atlantic Farm Women and their Historians." Agricultural History (1987): 61.

Kelly, G. M. "Work Demanded for Unemployed: Michigan Grange Told Jobs to Help Keep Us Out of War Should be Provided." Battle Creek News 1 November 1939.

King, C.W. Social Movements in the United States. New York: Random House, 1956.

Krout, John. New Outline—History of the United States since 1865. New York: Barnes & Noble, 1951.

Lahr, John. Automatic Vaudeville: Essays on Star Turns. New York: Limelight
Editions, 1985.

Larch, C. The American Family in Social-Historical Perspective. Ed. M. Gordon. New York: St. Martin's Press, 1983.

Laurie, Joe. Vaudeville: From the Honky-Tonks to the Palace. New York: Henry Holt, 1967.

Lease, Ruth. Creative Dramatics in Home, School, and Community. New York: Harper, n.d.

Lynes, Russell. The Lively Audience: A Social History of the Visual and Performing Arts in America 1890-1950. New York: Harper & Row, 1985.

MacGowan, Kenneth and W. Melnitz. The Living Stage. New York: Prentice Hall, 1955.

MacGowan, Kenneth. Footlights Across America. New York: Harcourt, Brace, 1929.

MacKaye, Percy. Community Drama: Its Motive and Method of Neighborliness. Boston: Houghton Mifflin, 1917.

—. The Civic Theatre In Relation to the Redemption of Leisure. New York: Little & Ives, 1912.

Mahoney, S. ""U" Honors First Woman Official with Marker." The State News 17 November 1987.

—. ""U" Honors First Woman Official With Marker." The State News 17 November 1987.

Manistee County Directory. Detroit: R.L. Polk & Co, 1895.

Manual of Subordinate Granges of the Patrons of Husbandry. 9th. Washington D.C.: National Grange, 1908.

Manual of Subordinate Patrons of Husbandry 9th edition. Philadelphia: George S. Derguson Company, 1908.

Marti, Donald B. To Improve the Soil and the Mind: Agricultural Societies, Journals and Schools in the Northeastern States 1791-1865. Ann Arbor, 1979.

—. Women of the Grange: Mutuality and Sisterhood in Rural America, 1866-1920. New York: Greenwood Press, 1991.

—. "Women's Work in the Grange: Mary Ann Mayo of Michigan 1882-1903." Agricultural History 1982: 439–452.

Martin, Theodora P. The Sound of Our Own Voices: Women's Study Clubs 1860-1910. Boston: Beacon Press, 1987.

Matkin, G.W. "Colleges as Promoters of Economic Development." Chronicle of Higher Education 17 November 1993: B1-2.

McCabe, James. History of the Grange Movement Or, the Farmer's War Against Monopolies. National Publishing, 1873.

McTeague, James H. Before Stanislavsky: American Professional Acting Schools and Acting Theory 1875-1925. Metuche: Scarecrow Press, 1993.

"Medics in Tribute to Dora Stockman." Michigan Patron 1939.

"Meet Mrs. Stockman, Only Woman Legislator." Detroit Free Press 1942.

Michigan House Journal. 1941.

Michigan House Journal. 1939.

Michigan House Journal. 1945.

"Michigan Legislator Cans: Michigan Cooking Apples..."

"Michigan Manual." Michigan Manual (1938): 224, 285.

"Michigan Progressive Republicans Go Forward." 1940.

Michigan State Grange Song Collection. Lansing: Dora Stockman, 1919.

Michigan State Grange Song Collection. Lansing: Dora Stockman, 1929.

Michigan State Grange Song Collection 3rd Edition. East Lansing: Dora Stockman, 1935.

Michigan State Grange Song Collection 5th edition. East Lansing: Dora Stockman, 1940.

"Michigan Women Backward in Taking Office." Detroit Free Press 14 August 1927.

Moeller, Ruby L. Easy Grange Programs. Boston: Bakers Plays, 1954.

Moles, L. "Woman Command Power in Politics." Lansing State Journal 1962.

Moody, Richard. America Takes the Stage. Bloomington: Indiana University Press, 1955.

Morgan, David. Suffragists and Democrats: The Politics of Woman Suffrage in America. East Lansing: Michigan State University Press, 1972.

Morgan, Wayne H., ed. The Gilded Age. Syracuse: Syracuse University Press, 1970.

"Mrs. Dora Stockman Leaves State Board." Michigan Patron 1931.

"Mrs. Stockman Has School Aid Bill." Lansing State Journal 1945.

Nel, Johanna. "Pioneers Responding to the Needs of Adult Students: Early Years at the University of Wyoming." J   of the West July 1993: 94-101.

Noll, Mark A. A History of Christianity in the United States and Canada. Grand Rapids: W. B. Erdman,   1992.

Nordin, Dennis S. Mainstreams of Grangerism: A Revisionist View of the Order of Patrons of Husbandry (1876-1900). Ph.D. Dissertation. Jackson: Mississippi State University, 1969.

—. Rich Harvest: A History of the Grange 1867-1900. Jackson: Mississippi University Press, 1974.

O'Rourke-Kelly, Margaret. American Agrarian Change Agent: The Dramatic Writings for Eudora Hall-Stockman for the Patrons of Husbandry. Ph.D. Dissertation. Minneapolis: Walden University,

1994.

O'Fritiof Ander. "The Immigrant Church of the Patrons of Husbandry." Agricultural History 8 October 1934: 155-158.

Patterson, Elizabeth H. "The Grange and Home Economics." The Journal of Home Economics (1913).

Paulsen, Gary. Farm: A History and Celebration of the American Farmer. Englewood Cliffs: Prentice Hall, 1977.

Poggi, Jack. Theater in America: The Impact of Economic Forces 1870-1967. Ithaca: Cornell University Press, 1968.

Prescott, G. "(Book Review) Knights of the Plow: Oliver H. Kelley and the Origins of the Grange in Republican Ideology." Agricultural History (1992): 377-378.

Program from Choral Performance. Perf. Benzonia College Choral Society. Benzonia College, Benzonia, Michigan. 1895.

"Progressive Republicans Go Forward." Campaign Material, 1 August 1938.

"Proposes Open Liquor State." Grand Rapids Press.

Quinn, Arthur H. A History of the American Drama: From the Civil War to the Present Day. New York: Appleton, Canbury, & Crofts, 1936.

Radio Talk. Perf. Dora Stockman. WJIM, East Lansing, Michigan. 6 November 1938.

"Real Grange Information: Especially Condensed for Busy Readers by National Secretary Caton." National Grange Monthly December 1941.

Reid, Daniel G. et al. Dictionary of Christianity in America. 1990.

"Resolution for Adequate Home Defense." 1939.

Rice, Stuartt A. Farmers and Workers in American Politics. New York : Columbia University, 1924.

Roberts, R. R. Popular Culture and Public Taste: The Guilded Age. Syracuse: Syracuse UP, 1970.

Robinson, William Louis. The Grange. The National Grange, 1966.

Rothman, Sheila M. Woman's Proper Place: A History of Changing Ideals and Practices, 1870 to the Present. New York: Basic Books, 1978.

"Roxburgh Retains Post as State Master." Bay City Daily News 1930.

Rugg, H.J. "Woman Legislator Would End State Liquor Monopoly." Lansing State Journal 1945.

Runnells, D. L. "Grange Bard Sets Records. Mrs. Dora H. Stockman has slept in more farm beds in Michigan than any other man or woman in the state." Grand Rapids Press 1936: 1.

Runnels, D.L. " 'Arm for Peace,' Woman Pleads at State Grange." The Grand Rapids Press 1 November 1939: 2.

—. "What's to Become of Mrs. Stockman?" Michigan Patron 6 November 1930.

Schnell, R.L. "History of Childhood as History of Education: A Review of Approaches and Sources." Alberta Journal of Educational Research (1979): 25.

Schnoebelen, Bill. "A Bible-based Look at the Grange." 1992. Saints Alive in Jesus. 4 May 1997 <http://www.saintsalive.com/freemasonry/grange.htm>.

Schwieder, D. "Education and Change in the Lives of Iowa's Farm Women, 1900-1940." Agricultural History (1986): 60.

Stock, Phyllis. Better Than Rubies: A History of Women's Education. New York: Knopf, 1978.

Stockman, Calvin and Judy. Personal Interview in Grand Rapids, Michigan M. O'Rourke. April 1998.

Stockman, Dora. A World Friendship Song. London: The National Grange and Associated Country Women of the World, 1936.

—. Cherry Harvest King. 1938.

Stockman, Dora. "Dr. Mary's Prescription." Book of Dialogs. Lansing: Henry R. Pattengill, 1913.

—. Farmerkins Farm Rhymes. Lansing, Michigan: Silver Burdette, 1911.

—. Farmerkins Farm Rhymes. Lansing: Pattengill, 1911.

—. Pageant. East Lansing: Michigan State University Archives and Historical Collection, 1934.

—. "Pageant-Grange Diamond Jubilee." University Archives and Historical Collection, 1941.

—. The Coming of Happy Valley Grange to Hard Scrabble Hollow. East Lansing: Michigan State University Archives and Historical Collection, n.d.

—. "The Grange and Rural Life in America." The Michigan Patron March 1942.

—. The Hope of Israel. East Lansing: Michigan State University Archives and Historical Collection, n.d.

—. The Story of Myself. East Lansing, Michigan, 1948.

—. Women in the Grange. Thesis. East Lansing: Michigan State University Archives and Historical Collection, 1930.

Stockman, Verne and Lucille. Personal Interview in Glen Arbor, Michigan M. O'Rourke. July 1985.

Stowell, S. A Stage of Their Own: Feminist Playwrights of the Suffrage Era. University of Michigan Press, 1992.

Taylor, Rosemary and John Case, Coops, Communes and Collectives: Experiments in Social Change in the 1960's and 1970's. New York: Pantheon Books, 1979.

Tetreau, Elzer Des Jardins. Farm Family Participation in Lodges, Grange, Farm Bureau, Four-H Clubs, School and Church: A Study of 610 Farm Families, Madison and Union Counties, Ohio, With Especial Attention to Owners and Tenants. University of Wisconsin, Ohio Agriculture Experiment Station, 1930.

"The Salt City of the Inland Seas." Manistee Daily News 31 October 1899, Anniversary number: Historical and Industrial Record of the Great Salt City ed.

"This Date in Michigan History." michiganhistorymagazine.com. 30 December 2006 <http://www.michiganhistorymagazine.com>.

Trump, Fred. The Grange in Michigan. Lansing: Fred Trump, 1963.

Vardac, Nicholas A. Stage to Screen: Theatrical Method from Garrick to Griffith. New York: Benjamin Blom, 1968.

Wallace, Irving and David Wallechinsky, "United States and American History: 1946." Trivial-Library.com. 12 November 2007. Reproduced from The People's Almanac , 1981. <http://www.trivia-library. com/a/united-states-and-american-history-1946.htm>

Warner, Estella Damon. The Story of the Grange: A Pageant. Massachusetts: Hampshire Country Pomona Grange, 1922.

Weatherford, D. American Woman's History. Englewood Cliffs, NJ: Prentice Hall, 1994.

Westley, F.C. "Place of Pageantry in National Thought." The Spectator 16 July 1906: 81-82.

Whitehead, M. The Origin and Progress of the Grange. New York: Patron's Paint Works, 1888.

Wiebe, Robert H. The Search for Order 1877-1920. New York: Hill and

Wang, 1967.

"Woman Lawmaker Decides to Retire." 1946.

"Women Legislators to be Seen More Than Heard this Session." 1938.

"Women Seek New Building: Farm Women Sign Petition to State Ag Board for Structure..." 31 July 1936.

"Women Speak Out About Themselves." AHA Perspectives (1983): 11-14.

Woods, E.R. "Chat with Contributors." Michigan Farmer and State Journal of Agriculture: The Household Supplement (1890): 4.

Woods, Thomas A. Knights of the Plow: Oliver H. Kelley and the Origins of the Grange in Republican Ideology. Ames: Iowa State University Press, 1991.

About the Author

MARGARET O'ROURKE-KELLY, PH.D. is a professor of communication and adult studies at Spring Arbor University. She is the co-author of Barnes Castle and author of Conversations with E.B. Pierce. Margaret created and  performs a one woman show based on the life and times of Dora Stockman. She has also written and performed radio commentary for public radio.

Margaret resides in Canton, Michigan with her delightful husband who offers unwavering support. She has two grown children who are a constant source of pleasure and inspiration.

It has been said that we read biographies to not only learn about the lives of others but to discover who we are and what we might become. I have long been interested in women's place in history. Dora Stockman is a rare find. It was the beginning of a journey that led me along her many pathways. She was the first woman elected to state-wide public office in Michigan. Among her many talents she was: an editor, educator, lyricist, poet, lecturer, playwright, politician, radio broadcaster, and reporter—all this activity while wife and mother. It was a moment of serendipity when I uncovered her rich, full life. My goal has been and will continue to be sharing the life and times of this amazing woman with others.

To order additional copies of *Phenomenal Woman: The Dora Stockman Story*, or to find out about other books by Margaret O' Rourke-Kelly, Ph.D. or Zoë Life Publishing, please visit our website www.zoelifepub.com.

A bulk discount is available when 12 or more books are purchased at one time.

Contact Outreach at Zoë Life Publishing:

Zoë Life Publishing
P.O. Box 871066
Canton, MI 48187
(877) 841-3400
outreach@zoelifepub.com

ZOË LIFE
PUBLISHING
WORDS TO LIVE BY